The GARDEN REVIVAL EXPERT

Dr. D. G. Hessayon

First edition: 80,000 copies

Published by Expert Books
a division of Transworld Publishers

A catalogue record for this book is available from the British Library

TRANSWORLD PUBLISHERS
61-63 Uxbridge Road, London W5 5SA
a division of the Random House Group Ltd

 Distributed in the United States
by Sterling Publishing Co. Inc.,
387 Park Avenue South,
New York,
NY 10016-8810

EXPERT BOOKS

Contents

Reproduction by Spot On Digital Imaging Ltd, Gomm Road, High Wycombe, Bucks HP13 7DJ
Printed and bound by Mohn Media Mohndruck GmbH

ISBN 0 903505 60 6

© D.G.HESSAYON 2004

CHAPTER 1

INTRODUCTION

You are not happy with the whole or just a part of your garden — that is why you bought this book. Maybe the shrubs and trees have become leggy and overgrown, or the lawn has become an eyesore. Maybe the climbers, once admired by the visitors, are now a tangled mass of stems, or the rockery is overrun with weeds.

There are several possible reasons why some or all of your garden is a disappointment to you. Maybe you have recently moved and had to take over someone else's neglect. Maybe you have just let things get out of hand or you simply want to look at something new. You are not alone. Gardens are living things and they all get old and tired unless they are tended regularly with care and skill. Even with this loving care some shrubs will be relatively short lived and no one ever avoids putting some plants in the wrong place.

It is straightforward when one of our rooms gets old and tired. A few rolls of paper, a few tins of paint or perhaps a few pieces of furniture and the room is renewed. It is not so easy with a garden.

Few of us have the time and even fewer have the money to begin all over again. If that's what you want to do then there are lots of books, videos, garden programmes and landscape architects to help you. What most of us want to do is to bring new life and restore lost beauty to the parts of the garden which we no longer find attractive. Some new planting may be necessary and you may have to change a feature or two, but usually we want to keep as much as we can. In simple words, we want to revive, renew or rejuvenate the garden.

We have a problem. Putting on a new coat of paint in the bedroom is a job which most of us have done over the years. If we haven't then there are lots of books and leaflets to show us what to do. Garden renewal is different. Doing the wrong things at the wrong time can be disastrous, but little has been written to show us what to do and for many people it is a task they have never had to tackle before. This book is designed to help you. You may well be skilled in annual maintenance pruning to keep trees, shrubs and roses in good condition, but renewal pruning is different. There is a price to pay — flowering is sometimes delayed or even lost for a season, but you will have restored shape to an eyesore. There are new things to learn.

The next chapter takes you on a trip around the garden to look at individual features. Here you may find an area which is bothering you — this might be a single tree or a group of plants. It might instead be a non-living item such as a badly-made rockery or a murky pond.

The third chapter deals with the general problems which may affect large areas of the garden. The trouble may be purely personal — the view may be felt to be dull or the garden is just too much work for you to do. On the other hand the problem may be a basic fault of the garden — weedy soil, large areas shaded by buildings or trees, poor plant growth in all the beds and borders etc.

Finally, there is a chapter on the basics of garden design with a step-by-step guide which takes you from a survey of the various styles available to the production of finished plans.

CHAPTER 2

SPECIFIC PROBLEMS

The call for action begins with a feeling of disappointment when you look at the garden. For some reason it is not as good as it used to be, or if you have just moved house it is not as good as you want it to be. The cause of this disappointment may be the overall appearance of the garden. There is a problem which seems to be affecting everything — shade, neglect, drought etc. This sort of problem is dealt with in the next chapter — here we are concerned with individual areas or plants which may need reviving, removal or replacing.

A garden may contain many elements, but there are three areas which stand out as major causes of an air of neglect. These are the overgrown tree, the overcrowded border and the poor-quality lawn.

The need for tree rejuvenation is more likely to occur in the larger garden where tall woody plants often play a dominant role. The usual problem is that the trees have grown into each other because of neglected or incorrect pruning and have become eyesores and/or too shady. It will be necessary to remove some of the specimens if they have been planted too closely together — renewal pruning will be needed if the overgrown trees are to remain.

Tree problems may be more pronounced in the larger garden but lawn problems can be more unsightly in the small garden than on the large estate. The reason is that the lawn is often the overwhelmingly dominant feature in the suburban back garden whereas in the larger wrap-around garden there are many distant features to distract the eye. Unfortunately you cannot expect any single product or technique to revive your lawn because there are many different causes of poor-quality turf and in most cases you will find that more than one culprit is responsible. It may be that the lawn is beyond saving and you will just have to start again, but you will probably find that you can bring the lawn back to the way it was by following a lawn renovation programme — see page 12.

The third area in this trio of eyesores is the overcrowded, poorly performing border of shrubs, bulbs and herbaceous perennials. Renewal pruning may help to restore neglected shrubs, but you do have to remember that some shrubs have a limited useful life span and replacement is necessary after a number of years. Trying to restore an old broom which has become lank and leggy is a waste of time. With herbaceous perennials there is a middle-age spread problem — the clumps expand each year and a stage is reached when the vigorous border plants start to swamp the more delicate ones, and these strong invasive growers develop a bare and ugly hollow heart. The answer is quite simple — you have to lift and divide these clumps every few years and replant pieces taken from the outer strong-growing section.

Trees, lawns and mixed borders are the common problem areas, but the list of trouble spots does not end there. There may be green slime in the pond, little or no fruit on the apple trees, a rockery which is overgrown or a vegetable plot which is an eyesore ... this chapter will show you what to do.

ROSES

Roses which give a disappointing display can pose a problem. Hard pruning, feeding and spraying should produce a dramatic improvement, but some old bushes and climbers may be simply worn out. Unfortunately, popping in a replacement plant is not an option.

THE WORN OUT ROSE

The plant may be obviously dead or there are just one or a few spindly shoots growing from a large and mature root stock. Flowering display has become increasingly poor over the years. Dead wood is usually abundant

Some varieties have a longer life span than others but all have a limit to their useful life. Modern varieties generally begin to deteriorate before they are 25 years old and a stage is reached when they are worn out.

The easiest thing to do is to dig out the plant and replace it with another type of shrub. The problem is that the exhausted plant may be part of a rose bed or you may be a rose lover who would not be satisfied with some other bush or climber. In this case you will have to replace the rose despite the fact that the soil will probably be rose sick. Follow the technique described below. Suspect a fatal disease (rose rust) or attack by honey fungus if the death of a previously vigorous plant has occurred quite quickly. Do not replant with a rose bush or climber.

Replacing old roses

Roses generally fail to thrive when planted in soil which has grown the same or a different variety for 10 years or more. This is because the new plant becomes affected by replant disease — a complex soil problem which is caused by the previous rose. There is no known cure.

If you plan to replace an old rose you should buy a container-grown and not a bare-root plant. Remove the old soil, digging out a hole which is 60 cm across and about 50 cm deep. Mix in plenty of compost with the soil in the bottom of the hole. Fill the space around the plant with soil from a part of the garden which has not grown roses. The old soil from the hole can be safely spread on flower beds or in the vegetable garden.

THE UGLY ROSE

Bush or climber with tall, woody and bare stems — in summer there is a crown of leaves and flowers. The general cause is neglected or faulty pruning — with climbers faulty training is an additional cause

A leafy bush in full flower or a climber clothed with blooms all along its stems is a splendid sight, but all too often we find a collection of ugly gaunt stems. A tip to try — remove a 10 mm x 3 mm horizontal strip of bark from a still-green bare stem and a bud below will break. However, hard pruning is generally required to produce new growth at a lower level. With climbing roses the new stems will need to be trained as shown below to ensure that flowers will continue to appear near the base as well as at the top of the plant. A year's floral display will be lost with ramblers, but the plant will be rejuvenated.

Renovating bushes

In March remove weak growth and cut back sturdy stems to about 15 cm above ground level. Remove weeds and break up the soil surface with a hand fork. In May apply a 5 cm deep mulch of compost or bark when the soil is moist.

The bush will nearly always survive this drastic treatment, but you won't see buds appear for several weeks if the stems are thick. When new growth does appear make sure that it is not a sucker arising from the rootstock.

In future years prune floribunda and hybrid teas by simply cutting away the top half off the stems in autumn or spring.

Renovating climbers

In March remove weak growth and cut back stems to about 15 cm above ground level. With vigorous ramblers cut back all the stems — with climbers cut back the oldest ones. New growth will appear and this must be properly trained — this will prevent the mature stems bearing their leaves and flowers only at the top. Do this by training the stem to be as horizontal as possible. Lateral branches will appear, and it is these laterals which grow upwards to provide both height and cover, and they bear the flowers.

With pillar roses wind the stems in an ascending spiral around the pole. Next season prune the climber or rambler in the standard way — see The Rose Expert.

THE SICK ROSE

Mildew is the most widespread disease, appearing in summer and early autumn

Black spot is a common and serious disease. Infection takes place early in the season, but it only becomes clearly visible in July/August

Several diseases can attack roses, but only two are both very common and very unsightly. Mildew and black spot can be controlled by spraying, but you have to begin early and repeat treatment is necessary. Remember to look for 'high disease resistance' on the label when buying new roses for your garden.

Rose rust (small dusty orange spots on the underside of the leaves) is the most serious disease as it can be fatal. Your plants are unlikely to be affected, but it is essential to spray with Systhane immediately if it does strike.

Die-back can be the reason why your bush has deteriorated. The trouble begins at the tip of a shoot and then progresses steadily downwards until the whole stem is killed. It can be caused by frost damage, canker at the base of the stem, waterlogging, mildew or black spot. Tackle it promptly — cut off the affected section at a bud below the dead area.

Tackling mildew

White powdery mould appears on leaves and flower buds. Leaves curl and fall prematurely, seriously weakening the plant and spoiling the display. It is encouraged by poor air circulation around the plant, inadequate feeding and by hot days which are followed by cold nights.

Apply Systhane at the first sign of disease. Repeat one week later and spray again if the spots reappear.

Tackling black spot

Black spots with yellow fringes spread rapidly on the leaves. Heavy infections spread to leaf buds and later to stems which die back. Severe defoliation may take place. It is encouraged by potash shortage and warm, wet weather in summer.

Black spot is difficult to control. Apply two sprays of Systhane a week apart when the leaf buds begin to open in spring. Spray again in summer when the first spots appear. Repeat as necessary. Remove fallen leaves.

LAWNS

An unsightly lawn is perhaps the most common cause of all gardening grumbles. There may be just one cause and a simple treatment is all that is required, but there is usually a number of problems and that calls for a renovation programme.

THE LAWN TO AIM FOR

Closely-knit turf with no patches of bare ground

Very little or no moss and no large patches of weeds. A light sprinkling of low-growing wild flowers such as daisies is acceptable — it is up to you

No serious lawn troubles — see pages 10-11 for the list

A bowling-green lawn may look attractive, but it is not what you should be aiming for. The luxury grade lawn needs a regular routine of feeding, weeding, aerating and top dressing — it will not stand heavy traffic and cutting is needed every few days in summer.

Aim instead for a hard-wearing utility grade lawn. This can thrive with ordinary weekend care and it will stand occasional neglect. This is the lawn for living with rather than looking at.

Stripes are not an indicator of quality. They are the result of the lawn being cut in parallel stripes by a mower fitted with a roller.

Luxury grade

Bent

Fescue

Turf and seed mixtures are made up of fine-leaved grasses. The broad-leaved grasses are not used, but may appear in mature lawns

Utility grade

Meadow grass

Ryegrass

Turf and seed mixtures are made up of broad-leaved grasses with the addition of one or more fine-leaved types such as Chewings Fescue

THE WORN OUT LAWN

Lawn grasses are absent. If they are present there is an overall sparse covering or a number of isolated patches

The surface is mainly covered with a mixture of moss, coarse grasses, unsightly weeds and bare earth

When a lawn has reached this sorry state there are only two alternatives. You can either continue to put up with it or you can start again. This calls for clearing the site of vegetation by spraying with glyphosate and then re-seeding or re-turfing. The Lawn Expert will show you how.

It often happens that only part of the lawn is in this worn-out state — the turf under a tree, the grass below a child's swing and the entrance of a frequently used grass path are common examples. Techniques for renovating a worn out lawn area are described below and repair kits are available at your garden centre, but be warned — it is difficult to blend the new patch into the surrounding turf.

Small patch renovation

Many things can cause the grass to die or disappear on a small patch of the lawn — compaction, bitch urine, under-tree drip, scalping of bumps by the mower etc. Always try to remedy the cause before carrying out the repair.

In spring or autumn clear away the top growth of weeds etc and either re-turf or re-seed as described below. Picking the right turf or seed is important — see the Renovation Programme on page 12.

Re-turfing

Remove dead patch and square up affected area. Break up soil surface and soil under the new turves with a hand fork — place in position. Firm down and fill in cracks with sifted soil.

Re-seeding

Prick the surface of the affected area with a fork. Rake to remove debris and to form a seed bed. Sow seed and cover area with a thin soil layer. Protect area from birds.

Large patch renovation

Overseeding is the way to deal with an extensive worn-out patch, and spring or summer when the soil is moist is the time to do it. Buy seed or a revival kit with a description of the grass type which is similar to the existing turf. Remove surface debris and rake to create a seed bed. Scatter the seed at the recommended rate and gently rake it in. Mow at a high setting when the grass is about 8 cm high — do not apply a weedkiller and/or mosskiller for about 6 months after sowing.

THE SECOND RATE LAWN

A reasonable cover of lawn grasses is present

The lawn has one or more of the problems described in the Rogues Gallery

Your first job is to find out what has caused the problem. It may have been faults at the lawn creation stage or perhaps neglect of the established turf by you or the previous owner. It may be due to doing the wrong thing, such as cutting too close or applying too much fertilizer/mosskiller. Finally it might be due to something beyond your control — disease, shade, moles etc.

Cure or remove the cause wherever you can and then overseed the affected area with a good quality seed mixture. It is not so simple if the whole lawn is in really poor condition. Here you should think about a full renovation programme — see page 12.

ROGUES GALLERY

• Disease

Diseases cause brown patches. They are much less widespread than the major pests (worms, moles and leatherjackets) but they can be more dangerous. Some like red thread are merely unsightly but ophiobolus patch can be a killer. If you feel that disease is the cause of your brown patches, send off a sample to an advisory service run by your gardening magazine or the Royal Horticultural Society.

• Leatherjackets

The worst of all insect pests, especially in heavy soil after a wet autumn. The 3 cm grey or brown grubs devour roots and stem bases in the spring — the grass turns yellow and brown. There is no chemical treatment. Water in the evening and spread a plastic sheet over the surface. Remove next morning and brush away the grubs.

• Bitch Urine

The brown patches are roughly circular in outline, with a ring of dark lush grass surrounding each patch. The effect is worst in dry weather. The problem is a difficult one — there are no effective repellents which can be used over the whole lawn, and the only thing you can do is to water the patches copiously. If one or more of the patches is an eyesore then re-seeding or re-turfing the area is the answer.

• Thatch

Thatch is a fibrous layer on top of the soil surface. When it is more than 3 cm thick it forms a semi-waterproof cover — downward passage of rain is restricted and aeration is impeded. Disease is encouraged and the turf begins to thin out. Scarify the surface with a lawn rake in autumn. You can hire a powered scarifier if the area is large.

• Moles

Mounds of earth appear overnight and long raised ridges may ruin the surface. All sorts of deterrents have been recommended — moth balls, smoke cartridges and so on, but they will return if they are not killed. Trapping is effective but it is a skilful task. The secret is to place the trap in a tunnel (probe down with a stick to find it) and disturb the area as little as possible. Poisoning is the best method — this job *must* be left to a professional mole-catcher.

• Earthworms

Worm casts can quite quickly ruin the surface. The casts are unsightly when flattened by the mower and the worms attract moles. Chemical wormkillers are no longer available and so you will have to rely on an annual dressing of a fertilizer which helps to acidify the soil — these are the quick-acting spring ones which contain sulphate of ammonia. Brush away dry casts before mowing.

• Weeds

Isolated weeds can be dealt with by hand weeding or treatment with a spot weedkiller, but an unsightly invasion over a large area calls for an overall treatment. There are the solid and liquid products containing one or more above selective weedkillers which do not harm grass. Mid April - late June is the best time for treatment. An alternative approach is to use a product containing ferrous sulphate. Unlike the selective ones these weedkillers are fast-acting, rapidly scorching broad-leaved weeds. They may burn the grass if over-applied and not watered in if the weather is dry.

• Toadstools

The usual cause is buried organic debris, and removing this will often eliminate a small clump of toadstools. Fairy rings are more serious — two dark green circles in the grass with a bare space in between. The ring grows wider every year and the usual cause is Marasmius — a brown-capped 5-10 cm high toadstool. Many cures have been proposed, but replacing the soil and re-turfing is the only satisfactory answer. A lot of work — the usual approach is to live with the problem.

• Moss

There is no simple answer — it is necessary to follow a season-long programme. In spring apply a lawn feed/weed/mosskiller product containing ferrous sulphate — if the patch is not large you can spray with a ready-to-use dichlorophen product. Rake out the dead moss a few weeks later and re-seed any bare patches. Feed the lawn in early summer and mow regularly at the recommended height — closely shaving the lawn is a common cause of moss infestation. Remove the cause of shade if possible and rake in autumn. Spike to improve drainage.

• Broken Edges

Cut out a square of turf carrying the broken edge. Use a spade to prise up the cut square and move it forward so that the damaged part projects beyond the border. Now trim to line up with the rest of the lawn. Use the piece you have removed to fill the gap at the back of the square of turf. Put soil in the hollow area, firm down and sow with grass seed.

• Bumps & Hollows

Do not try to roll out bumps — the area will become more unsightly than ever. Remove the bump by cutting the grass and rolling back the turf above the affected area. Remove soil to level the surface — roll back the turf and fill cracks with sifted soil. Small hollows can be gradually filled in by working sifted soil (no more than 1 cm thickness at a time) into the turf at regular intervals. Deep hollows call for surgery as described above, adding rather than removing soil.

• Pale Grass

A pale green or yellowish look usually indicates a lack of nitrogen. Mowing is a serious drain on the soil's reserve of this element, and unless it is replaced the turf becomes thin and sparse. Feeds based on sulphate of ammonia give rapid green-up, but are not long-lasting. Slow-acting ones work for months, but do not expect a quick change in colour. Feed when the soil is moist and the surface is dry. Use a fertilizer distributor for an even spread and water in if it doesn't rain for 2 days. Do not use a high nitrogen fertilizer in autumn.

Moles

Earthworms

Weeds

Toadstools

LAWN RENOVATION PROGRAMME

A neglected lawn is a depressing sight. You may have moved into a house which has been vacant for some time or you may have been unable to look after your own lawn because of absence, sickness etc. Whatever the reason your first job will be to carefully examine the grass and weeds. If weeds and moss dominate and there are only wisps of lawn grasses, then you have a worn out lawn and the best plan is to start again — see page 9. In most cases the desirable lawn grasses will be found to make up most of the lawn. Remaking the lawn is not necessary here — follow the renovation programme described below. Note that an unsightly neglected lawn cannot be transformed overnight — it will take a whole season and a number of different tasks.

❶ Cut down the tall grass and weeds to about 5 cm from the ground. Only use a scythe if you are skilled in the art — it is better to hire a large strimmer. Spring is the best time to start this renovation programme. Remove all the cut vegetation with a rake and then brush the surface. Remember that anything which can harm the mower must be removed.

❷ Re-examine the lawn surface. Use the Rogues Gallery on pages 10-11 or the more complete catalogue in The Lawn Expert to list the lawn troubles which are present. These problems must be tackled at the recommended time and in the recommended way.

❸ Mow with the blades set as high as possible. Trim the edges after this first cut — create a narrow bare mowing strip between the lawn and walls. Over the next few weeks progressively lower the height of cut to 2.5 - 3 cm. Cut at weekly intervals.

❹ Feed and weed the lawn in early summer using a combined dressing through a wheeled distributor. Be careful not to overdose.

❺ Water in summer and feed if necessary in autumn. Water thoroughly in prolonged dry weather. Use an autumn lawn fertilizer (low nitrogen) in September if the turf is pale.

❻ Shortly afterwards carry out lawn repairs. Remove bumps and hollows, repair broken edges etc — see page 11.

❼ A little later spike compacted areas and overseed if necessary. Seed all bare patches and thin grass areas with the appropriate mix (shady mixture for under trees, drought mixture for sandy soil etc). Fine-leaved meadow grass is now available.

❽ Next spring begin a normal lawn management programme. See The Lawn Expert for details.

PERENNIALS

THE BORDER TO AIM FOR

Perhaps you have decided to renew your herbaceous border — a long strip filled only with perennials. Consider turning it into a mixed border where the herbaceous perennials share the ground with shrubs, bulbs etc. In this way you will have year round interest rather than a plot which is almost bare from late autumn to mid-spring.

The bare ground between the plants has been mulched in late spring — see page 78 for details. Mulching and vigorous plant growth should keep weeds under control — hoe or hand-pull any unwanted growth as it appears

The clumps may touch but vigorous types are not allowed to crowd out smaller gems. Overcrowding is avoided by not planting too closely, dividing plants when they become invasive and by removing self-sown seedlings when they begin to transgress

Tall and weak-stemmed plants are staked — this has been done when the plants were still quite small and this has allowed leafy growth to cover the staking material. Never use a single cane for bushy plants — put in several supports and hold in stems with twine or raffia

The classic border has 3 basic rows. Tall plants form the back row and the dwarfs are at the front — between them are the middle-border plants. Don't stick slavishly to this formula of a constant slope — break it by having an occasional tall plant close to the front

The mixed border has taken over from the all-perennial herbaceous border in most home gardens. Out-of-season interest is created by adding compact conifers, coloured-leaf evergreens, bulbs etc. A few winter- and early spring-flowering perennials (Helleborus, Polyanthus, Viola odorata, Bergenia etc) can be added to ensure year-round interest

Labelling is useful but not essential. It is a great help to know the names of the plants when clump division is planned for the spring when top growth is absent

The plants are grown in groups or drifts rather than as single specimens of a wide range of varieties. Shrubs and large showy perennials are exceptions to this rule

BEGINNING FROM SCRATCH

Front row plants in groups of 5
Middle row plants in groups of 4
Back row plants in groups of 3
Plant large architectural plants
(e.g Cortaderia) singly

There are times when we may decide to clear the border and start again. The usual reason is the presence of a sea of grassy and broad-leaved weeds between the plants. Neglect by you or the previous occupant is the cause and there is no point in just clearing away the weeds — they will soon return and weeding becomes a never-ending job. Another reason may be that you have got tired of the display or you may have moved into a new house and you want to create your own feature. Follow the 7 steps below and remember not to plant too closely. Leave 20-30 cm between front row plants, 45 cm between middle row plants and 60 cm between back row plants.

7 STEPS TO REMAKING THE BORDER

STEP 1 Choose the right season and the right day. Spring or autumn is the time to choose and the soil should be moist when you start to plant.

STEP 2 Remove any plants you want to keep. Divide (see page 16) if necessary and pot up or plant in a nursery bed for later use. Take the opportunity to remove any weeds growing in the clump.

STEP 3 Prepare the soil. This is a vital stage — treat the surface with glyphosate if it is weedy and dig if necessary. Incorporate organic matter into the soil. Let the soil settle for a couple of weeks before you start planting.

STEP 4 Make your list. Never create a herbaceous border by wandering around the garden centre and picking plants at random because you like the picture on the label. Look through a comprehensive picture guide and choose the shrubs and perennials which suit your situation (soil type, shade, space etc) as well as for their personal appeal. Look at flowering times — aim for spring, summer and autumn colour. Pick most of the plants from the easy-care list on page 15 if you want a low maintenance bed.

STEP 5 Prepare a plan. Draw up a plan — see Chapter 4. Follow the spacing and number of plants per station rules shown above. You can repeat a variation of the pattern if length permits or you can have two or more stations of a single variety next to each other.

STEP 6 Buy the plants. Wherever possible buy plants which you can inspect before buying. Look for specimens with healthy, undamaged leaves growing in moist compost. It is usually wise to avoid plants which are in flower. It may be possible to divide up a large specimen — see page 16.

STEP 7 Plant properly.

Planting a container-grown perennial can take place at any time of the year provided the soil is neither frozen nor waterlogged, but choose either spring or autumn if you can. With small plants the hole is usually filled with the soil which has been removed. With large plants it is better to use a planting mixture of 1 part topsoil, 1 part moist peat and 3 handfuls of Bone Meal per barrowload

② Water the pot or container thoroughly at least an hour before planting. Remove the plant very carefully — do not disturb the soil ball. With a pot-grown plant place your hand around the crown of the plant and turn the pot over. Gently remove — tap the sides with a trowel if necessary

④ After planting there should be a shallow water-holding basin. Water in after planting

① The hole should be deep enough to ensure that the top of the soil ball will be about 3 cm below the soil surface after planting. The hole should be wide enough for the soil ball to be surrounded by a layer of planting mixture — twice as wide as the soil ball is the recommendation. Put a 3 cm layer of planting mixture at the bottom of the hole

③ Examine the exposed surface — cut away circling or tangled roots but do not break up the soil ball. Fill the space between the soil ball and the sides of the hole with planting mixture. Firm down the planting mixture with your hands

EASY-CARE BORDER PERENNIALS

Fully hardy. Not prone to disease. No staking. No need to divide every few years

NAME	SITE	HEIGHT RANGE	FLOWERING TIME
ACHILLEA	Sun	60 cm - 1.2 m	June - Sept
AJUGA	Sun or light shade	15 cm	April - June
ALCHEMILLA	Sun or light shade	20 - 45 cm	June - July
ANEMONE	Sun or light shade	60 cm - 1.2 m	Aug - Oct
ARUNCUS	Light shade	90 cm - 1.8 m	June - July
ASTILBE	Light shade	60 - 90 cm	July - Aug
BERGENIA	Sun or light shade	30 cm	March - April
COREOPSIS	Sun	30 - 60 cm	July - Oct
DICENTRA	Light shade	30 - 60 cm	May - June
DORONICUM	Sun or light shade	30 - 90 cm	April - June
EUPHORBIA	Sun or light shade	10 cm - 1.5 m	April - May
GERANIUM	Sun or light shade	15 - 60 cm	July - Sept
HELLEBORUS	Partial shade	30 - 60 cm	Jan or March
HEMEROCALLIS	Sun or light shade	60 - 90 cm	June - Aug
HEUCHERA	Sun or light shade	40 - 60 cm	June - Aug
HOSTA	Partial shade	30 - 60 cm	June - Aug
IRIS	Sun	30 - 80 cm	Depends on species
NEPETA	Sun	20 - 60 cm	May - Sept
PRIMULA	Partial shade	30 - 60 cm	Depends on species
PULMONARIA	Partial shade	30 - 40 cm	April - May
RUDBECKIA	Sun or light shade	60 cm - 1.5 m	July - Oct
SEDUM	Sun	30 - 60 cm	Aug - Oct
SOLIDAGO	Sun	30 cm - 1.8 m	July - Sept
TRADESCANTIA	Sun or light shade	45 - 60 cm	June - Sept

Doronicum plantagineum

Geranium pratense

Hemerocallis 'Stafford'

THE OVER-AGED PERENNIAL

A hollow heart is the usual sign of old age, but not all border perennials develop a dead central area as they get older. The feature all over-aged perennials have in common is unattractive growth and a failure to flower as freely as in previous seasons

A few perennials are relatively short-lived — Anchusa, Aquilegia, Linum etc and so they do not usually reach an over-age stage. At the other end of the scale are many of the easy-care group listed on page 15 which can go on and on for years without any sign of old age.

For most border perennials it is a different story. After about four or five years the floral display begins to deteriorate and so lifting, dividing and replanting are necessary to restore the earlier vigour — see below for details.

Division and replanting may be necessary with a perennial which is still vigorous and free-flowering. The problem here is that the clump has begun to encroach on its more delicate neighbour and so action is necessary to bring it under control.

Lifting & dividing border perennials

Always check in the A-Z guide of The Flower Expert before lifting a perennial. Some plants hate disturbance. Choose a mild day when the soil is moist. Dig up the clump with a fork. Shake off the excess soil and study where the basic divisions should be. You might be able to break the clump with your hands — if the clump is too tough then use two hand forks or garden forks. Push the forks back-to-back into the centre and prise gently apart. Treat the resulting divisions in a similar fashion or tear apart with the fingers. Select the divisions from the outer region of the clump — remove any weeds.

(4) Plant properly. Fill around the soil ball with loose soil and firm with the fingers or the trowel handle. Water in after planting

(3) Plant at the right depth. Use the old soil mark on the stem as your guide

(2) Use the right tool. A trowel is generally the best thing to use

(1) Dig the hole to fit the roots. The hole should be much wider than it is deep

THE FLOWER-SHY PERENNIAL

This specimen of Convolvulus cneorum has kept the silvery sheen on its foliage but very few flowers have appeared — the problem is the dense shade cast by the surrounding shrubs

The perennials in your border should provide an impressive sight in summer with a mass of attractive flowers. That is what you see in the show gardens you visit, but in your own garden the plants may fail to produce this abundance of blooms. Unfortunately there is no single cause. There are many reasons why a perennial may be flower-shy — listed below are the most likely causes. To find the reason, ask these questions. Are all the plants in the border giving poor results (poor soil, drought etc)? Are just a few plants affected (poor plant choice, pests, diseases etc)? Has the plant steadily deteriorated (old age etc)?

The basic rules are to choose good specimens of plants which are right for the situation, put them in properly prepared soil, feed with a potash-rich fertilizer in spring and pinch out stem tips of bushy perennials when they are about 15 cm high.

WHY PLANTS FAIL TO FLOWER PROPERLY

• Impatience
A recently-planted perennial may not bloom in the first season after planting. Some border plants such as peonies hate being moved.

• Too much shade
Some perennials demand a sunny site. Always check the light requirements of any plant you propose to buy.

• Pests and diseases
A number of insects and fungal diseases can kill or distort flowers — see The Flower Expert for identification.

• Old age
Plants can deteriorate with age. The answer is to lift and divide — see page 16 for details.

• Too little water
Drought results in a sub-standard display if you fail to water. Apply a mulch in late spring. Water in dry weather before the leaves start to suffer.

• Late frost
A late frost can kill the buds on plants which are not fully hardy. Avoid plants which are known to be slightly tender if you live in a hard-winter area. You can protect a semi-hardy plant when frost is forecast by draping horticultural fleece over the stems.

• Poor feeding
The plants may be hungry. The feed to use is one with a potash (K) content higher than the nitrogen (N) one — the pack will have this information.

ROCKERY

THE ROCKERY TO AIM FOR

A rockery which has been properly made, imaginatively planted and well tended can be one of the highlights of a garden, but all too often it is a stony eyesore. It may have been badly constructed in the first place or it may have been neglected. When both these problems are present then you will have to start again (see page 19) to incorporate the features shown below.

The whole of the rock garden is made up of one type of rock — sandstone and second-hand limestone are the popular choices. Broken concrete and reconstructed stone are not used

The structure looks like a natural outcrop of sloping rocks, made up of large and small stones. Ideally the rockery faces south or west and there is some protection from northern winds

Slow-growing delicate plants such as gentian and penstemon are planted well away from invasive mat-forming types such as aubretia and snow-in-summer. Weeds are regularly removed

There can be trees growing nearby, but there are no overhanging branches above the rockery — a blanket of leaves over delicate plants in autumn can be fatal. The site should be free from shade for most of the day — ferns and other shade-tolerant plants are grown in the less sunny areas

The bare ground between the plants and under the leaves is covered with a 2-3 cm layer of fine gravel, stone chippings or grit. This layer deters slugs, conserves moisture, helps to suppress weeds and gives a more natural look to the rockery. This gritty mulch is topped up each spring

Most rock plants need soil that is free draining but also water retentive — this calls for the addition of both gritty material and organic matter. It is not usually practical to enrich all of the soil in the rockery — it is more usual to use a planting mixture (page 21) and not ordinary soil for filling the holes around new plants

A wide selection of plants are present. Most are rockery perennials (no clear-cut definition — they are the plants in the alpine section of the garden centre). Also present are one or more dwarf conifers (Pinus mugo 'Gnom', Picea mariana 'Nana' etc), dwarf shrubs, dwarf bulbs and ferns

BEGINNING FROM SCRATCH

There are two reasons why you may want to build and plant a rockery from scratch. It may be that you have decided to have one in your garden for the first time. Or you may have a rock garden but it was badly made (page 20) and has become distinctly unattractive with its cover of weeds and rampant rockery plants. Whatever the reason, follow the steps below.

5 STEPS TO BUILDING A ROCKERY

STEP 1 Plan carefully. Your first job is to learn how a sloping outcrop should look. The drawing on the right should give you some idea — visit a good rock garden or two and take photographs. Look up Stone Merchants in Yellow Pages and ask for samples and quotes. Visit and select your own stones if possible. Choose sizes in the 10-100 kg range — pick weathered pieces. A 3 m x 2 m rock garden will require 1½ -2 tonnes of rock.

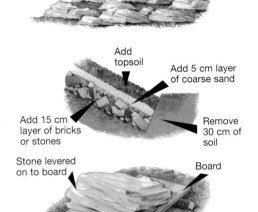

Sloping Outcrop

STEP 2 Prepare the site. With a virgin site strip off any turf which may be present. If the site is an existing rockery it will be necessary to dig out and pot up any plants you wish to keep before moving the stones to a holding area. The next step is weed removal. Dig out the roots — if badly infested use glyphosate. Good drainage is another vital need. With a sloping site in a non-clayey area no extra preparation will be required, but if the subsoil is heavy the creation of a drainage layer (see illustration) is recommended.

Add topsoil

Add 5 cm layer of coarse sand

Add 15 cm layer of bricks or stones

Remove 30 cm of soil

STEP 3 Move the stones. You will be able to move small stones by simply carrying them. Wear leather gloves and stout boots. With help you should be able to tackle rocks weighing 25 kg in this way, but in a large rockery you will need some much larger stones. For medium-sized rocks use a sack trolley — you will have to lay down a trackway of boards on soft ground. Do not use a single-wheeled barrow as the load can easily tip over. Some stones may be too large for a sack trolley — use the technique shown on the right.

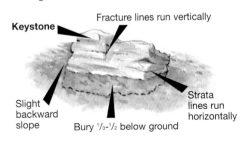

Stone levered on to board

Board

Rollers (rustic poles)

Slowly push the structure along, moving the back roller to the front

STEP 4 Lay the keystone. You will need a crowbar, spade, some wooden planks, a stout stick for ramming soil between the stones and one or more capable helpers. Ideally there should be a gentle slope of about 10° — if the site is flat you will need about 1 tonne of top soil for every 2 sq.m. Look at the stones and choose one which is large and has an attractive face — this will be the keystone which will serve as the centre point for the first tier of stones. Dig out a hollow which is larger than the base of the keystone and roll this rock into place. Use the crowbar to lever it into its final position. Push rubble under this keystone and add planting mixture (see page 21) both under and behind it. Ram this down firmly with a stick.

Fracture lines run vertically

Keystone

Slight backward slope

Bury ⅓-½ below ground

Strata lines run horizontally

STEP 5 Lay the rest of the stones. Follow step 4 with stones of various sizes on either side of the keystone — this will complete the first tier. Some stones should be pushed tightly together using the crowbar but avoid a continuous line one stone high. It is better to arrange the stones in groups. Now move on to the second tier of stones — it may be necessary to put down wooden plank ramps. Continue until all the stones have been set in position. The last step is to add more planting mixture, let it settle for a few weeks and then start planting — see page 21.

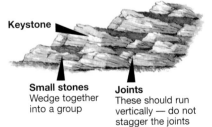

Keystone

Small stones
Wedge together into a group

Joints
These should run vertically — do not stagger the joints

THE BADLY MADE ROCKERY

The 'currant bun' rockery is a mound of earth with a scatter of round flat stones dotted over the surface

The 'dogs graveyard' rockery is a mound of earth with a series of oblong stones standing upright on the surface

Currant bun or dogs graveyard — a badly made rockery has a wholly artificial look and does not provide an attractive background for alpines and other rockery plants. To put it right you will have to dig up and pot any plants you want to keep, move the stones to give the appearance of a natural outcrop and then plant up with new and saved specimens — see page 19 for details.

Unfortunately remaking a rockery is never easy, especially if you don't have enough stones of the right type or if it looks like a charmless island in the middle of a flat lawn. If you are fond of rockery plants but are daunted by the idea of making or remaking a rockery, you can consider creating a raised alpine bed — it is an easier, cheaper and less space-demanding alternative to make and a less time-consuming area to maintain.

Creating a raised alpine bed

A height of 50 cm-1 m is recommended and the retaining walls can be made with bricks, stone, reconstituted stone blocks or railway sleepers. Where space permits an upper terrace or a series of terraces can be built on the bed to create extra interest and a place for trailing plants. Clear away perennial weeds before you begin and lay a concrete foundation if the walls are to be more than 30 cm high. Leave weep-holes at the base if mortar-bonded bricks, blocks or stones are the building material.

When the walls are finished, add a layer of bricks, rubble or stones if the soil below is not free draining. Cover with grit and fill with standard planting mixture — see page 21. Leave a 5 cm space between the surface and the top of the retaining wall and wait a few weeks before introducing the plants. Top up if necessary. Choice and planting technique are the same as for the rock garden — the use of trailing types to partially cover the top of the retaining wall is especially important. Cover the soil with a 3 cm layer of stone chippings.

THE OVERGROWN ROCKERY

Vigorous mat-forming perennials have swamped most or all of the more delicate alpines

Weeds are growing around and within the clumps of rockery perennials

Leave a shrub border untended for a year and no great harm may result, but treat a rockery in this way and it will almost certainly become an eyesore which will require a lot of work to put right. Listed below are the steps required to restore an overgrown rockery. Once restored make sure that you carry out routine maintenance. Once a week you should weed, trim, clear debris and water when necessary, and then a major overhaul in spring and autumn when replanting, cutting back, mulching etc is carried out — see The Rock & Water Garden Expert for details.

Some replanting will be necessary on occasions in even the best kept rockery as the attractive life span of many alpines is 5-8 years, after which they need to be lifted, divided and then replanted — see below for details.

Restoring the overgrown rockery

Remove all surface rubbish and cut back all overgrown carpeting perennials — dig out all dead plants. Weed control is essential — pull out all annual weeds and self-sown alpines growing in the wrong place. Perennial weeds are a difficult problem when the roots are too deep to be removed — the answer is to paint the leaves very carefully with glyphosate gel. When the weeds are growing within the clump it will be necessary to lift, divide, carefully pull away the weeds and their roots and then replant as described below. Make up a planting mixture of 1 part topsoil, 1 part grit and 1 part peat or well-rotted leaf mould. It is now time for planting. Leave the good specimens, divide up old clumps and buy pots of new specimens. Plan to cover some but not all the rock faces with carpeting plants and aim for year-round colour.

Dig a hole which is clearly larger than the soil ball and fill with water. When it has drained away put in the root ball and fill the space around it with planting mixture. Firm the mixture with your fingers and water in. Cover the surface with grit or stone chippings.

VEGETABLES

There is a decision to be made if you have a run-down vegetable plot. If you are keen on growing vegetables and want to carry on with the long-row allotment style you are used to, then set about improving it as described below. If, on the other hand, you want to find an easier method of growing vegetables then the bed system (pages 24-25) could be the answer. It may be that you want a vegetable plot which is an attractive and colourful feature rather than a utility one — then consider the potager (page 23). Finally, the answer is simple if you are not interested in growing food crops — use the land for something else.

THE TRADITIONAL PLOT

The standard way of growing vegetables. Plants are grown in long rows with strips of bare earth between them. Satisfying for some, but a muddy chore in wet weather for others

The best method for producing top-size vegetables, but it is time-consuming. The pathways and large spaces between plants encourage weeds, and the plot has to be dug over each autumn or winter

Improving the traditional plot

Restoration should begin in late autumn or early spring. Before you lift a spade draw a plan — buy a reference book such as The Vegetable & Herb Expert to guide you. Do think about crop rotation when drawing up your plan — the standard 3-year plan may be too complex for you, but you can follow the simple rule of a patch of root vegetables one year and above-ground vegetables on it next year.

Begin by digging in well-rotted manure if the land is starved. Take time and care when making the seed bed and mark out each row with a length of taut string. Remember the golden rules — sow not too early, not too deeply and not too thickly. The supports put in for climbers must be stout enough for a heavy crop — a series of wigwams made up of bamboo canes is an attractive alternative to the more usual row of stakes. There are three vital routines to prevent the plot developing a run-down look as the season progresses. Hoe regularly to keep down weeds, take action against pests and diseases as soon as they appear and pick or cut vegetables when they are ready whether or not you can use them. Leaving unwanted vegetables to go to seed will spoil the look of any vegetable garden.

THE POTAGER

A section of the garden containing a geometric pattern of beds divided by permanent paths. The beds are often enclosed by dwarf hedging

The main component of the beds is an assortment of vegetables, but one or more other types of plants are included — herbs, fruit trees and bushes, flowers, roses and bulbs

'Potager' is the French word for kitchen garden, but in this country it has a more specialised meaning. It is basically a vegetable plot, but there are two special features. Firstly, it is strictly formal — the beds are usually square or rectangular, but they can be round or oval. The beds should be compact enough to allow easy access from the pathways. The pathways between the beds are made of paving slabs or gravel, and archways draped with roses, beans, grapes etc are sometimes constructed along the paths.

The second key feature is that the ornamental aspect of the vegetables, herbs and fruit which are grown is just as important as their value in the kitchen. Colourful vegetable varieties are usually chosen in preference to the plain varieties and tree fruit is often grown as pyramids or cordons. Apart from the eye-catching types of vegetables some ordinary types can look attractive in the right setting — there are the ferny leaves of carrots and the yellow flowers of courgettes. To heighten the ornamental aspect a variety of flowers, roses and shrubs may be included, but these should be kept in the background.

A word of warning. A potager can be an outstanding feature in the garden but the mixture of annual, biennial and perennial plants requires regular attention if the ornamental vegetable garden is not to acquire a run-down look.

COLOURFUL POTAGER VEGETABLES

Aubergine – Bambino
    – Black Enorma
Brussels sprout – Rubine
Cabbage – Red Drumhead
    – Ruby Ball
Capsicum – Gypsy
    – Redskin
French bean – Kinghorn Wax
    – Purple Podded

Globe artichoke
Leaf beet – Ruby Chard
    – Swiss Chard
Lettuce – Lollo Rossa
Rhubarb
Runner bean – Hestia
    – Painted Lady
    – White Lady
Tomato – Yellow Perfection

Tomato – Yellow Perfection

THE BED SYSTEM

A series of rectangular beds are separated by permanent paths. Care is much simpler than with the traditional plot method

Dwarf or early-maturing varieties are usually chosen — they are grown closely together (see page 25) so that leaves of adjacent plants touch when mature

The bed system has several distinct advantages compared with the standard allotment pattern. The close spacing results in most weeds being smothered and the gravel- or bark-covered paths mean that there are no muddy walkways. Perhaps the most important advantage is that annual digging is not necessary.

The yearly round begins in autumn or early winter when a layer of organic matter such as rotted manure or garden compost is worked into the surface with a fork. Sowing and planting take place in the usual way, but the row spacing and plant spacing are the same. Yields per sq.m are higher than you would obtain by the traditional plot method, but the size of each individual vegetable is usually smaller.

Making the bed

The diagram below is a general guide to the dimensions to aim for — note that the beds are narrow enough to allow all the plants to be reached from the paths. If possible construct the beds so that they run north to south.

The flat bed as illustrated in the photograph above is the easier type to construct but you do need free-draining soil. Use the dimensions given for raised beds in the drawing. Turn the soil over and work in a 3 cm layer of organic matter. Let it settle for at least a couple of weeks before sowing or planting.

The raised bed is the type to make if drainage is poor. You will have to build retaining walls — railway sleepers, bricks or reconstituted stone blocks can be used, but stout planks with square wooden posts at the corners are the usual choice. The raised bed should be at least 10 cm high — fork over the bottom and then fill with a mixture of 2 parts topsoil and 1 part organic matter.

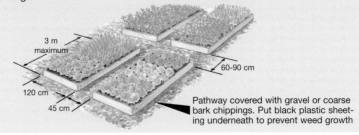

3 m maximum

60-90 cm

120 cm

45 cm

Pathway covered with gravel or coarse bark chippings. Put black plastic sheeting underneath to prevent weed growth

EASY-CARE VEGETABLES FOR THE BED SYSTEM

NAME	SOW	DEPTH	PLANT	DISTANCE * BETWEEN PLANTS	HARVEST	TIME ** TAKEN (weeks)
BEAN, BROAD	February — April	5 cm	—	15 cm	July — August	16S → H
Favourite varieties include 'Aquadulce' and 'Bunyard's Exhibition' — the favourite dwarf is 'The Sutton'. Begin picking when pods are 7.5 cm long — cook whole						
BEAN, FRENCH	May — June	5 cm	—	15 cm	July — September	10S → H
The popular Flat-podded or English varieties tend to become stringy as they mature. The Pencil-podded or Continental varieties (e.g 'Sprite') are stringless						
BEETROOT	April — June	2.5 cm	—	8 cm	June — October	11S → H
Grow a globe variety — harvest when no larger than a tennis ball. Reliable varieties include 'Boltardy', 'Monopoly' and 'Monodet'						
CARROT	March — July	1 cm	—	10 cm	July — October	14S → H
Pick a quick-maturing short-rooted variety such as the round 'Early French Frame' or the finger-long 'Amsterdam Forcing'						
COURGETTE	May — June	2.5 cm	—	45 cm	July — September	10S → H
Courgettes are marrows cut at the immature stage when 7.5-10 cm long. Varieties include 'Gold Rush' (yellow) and 'Defender' (green)						
KALE	May	1 cm	July	40 cm	December	30S → H
'Pentland Brig' is the variety to grow. Pick young leaves in winter, young shoots in early spring and spears (cook like broccoli) a little later						
LETTUCE	March — July	1 cm	—	25 cm	June — October	12S → H
Grow a Miniature e.g 'Tom Thumb' or 'Little Gem' or a loose-leaf variety (e.g 'Salad Bowl') — a few leaves can be removed each time over many weeks						
ONION	—	Tip showing	March — April	8 cm	August	20P → H
Grow sets rather than seed — harvest 2 weeks after stems topple over. Popular varieties include 'Stuttgarter Giant' and 'Sturon'						
POTATO	—	12.5 cm	March — April	30 cm	June — July	13P → H
Grow an early variety for new potatoes in early summer — examples include 'Arran Pilot', 'Foremost', 'Pentland Javelin' and 'Sharpe's Express'						
RADISH	March — July	1 cm	—	5 cm	May — September	6S → H
Nothing is easier to grow. There are many varieties —— e.g 'Cherry Belle' (round/red), 'Sparkler' (round/white-red) and 'Large White Icicle' (long/white)						
SPINACH BEET	April	2.5 cm	—	20 cm	August — November	15S → H
This type of leaf beet is similar to spinach but it is not prone to bolting and the leaves are larger and fleshier						
TOMATO	—	—	June	45 cm	August — September	12P → H
An easy crop, but only if you choose a bush variety such as 'The Amateur' and grow it in a warm, sunny and sheltered spot						
TURNIP	March — June	1 cm	—	15 cm	May — September	10S → H
Early or bunching varieties (e.g 'Snowball') are sown early in the year and picked at golf-ball size for salads or stews						

* DISTANCE BETWEEN PLANTS
These spacings are the recommended distance between the rows and also between the mature plants in the rows

** TIME TAKEN (weeks)
S: Sowing
P: Planting
→ : to
H: Harvest

BULBS

THE DISPLAY TO AIM FOR

Crocuses and snowdrops followed by daffodils and tulips are the heralds of spring in millions of gardens. With care your bulbs will multiply over the years, but with poor handling the stock may rapidly deteriorate. The rules are easy to follow.

Most of the bulbs we buy are the spring flowering ones. A few summer flowering ones such as gladioli are also popular, but the range of bulbs we grow is surprisingly small. Add interest by planting some autumn Cinderellas such as montbretia and kaffir lily

There are no fixed rules about the arrangement of bulbs in beds and borders, but it is generally agreed that most bulbs look best when grown in informal groups rather than in regular-spaced neat rows. The exceptions are large-flowered tulips and gladioli

Depth of planting is important — see page 27. If the bulb is too shallow there is a danger of frost damage in winter and buds cracking in a hot summer. Plant too deeply and there is a likelihood that the plant will not develop properly

Some but not all bulbs have to be dug up each year after flowering and are then stored in the dormant state for replanting. There is no need to dig up daffodils in this way every year, but there are times when you should do this — see page 28. The usual practice with garden tulips is to lift them every year when the foliage has turned yellow and then store them in a frost free place for replanting in November. However, if you cover the bulbs with 15-20 cm of soil at planting time you should be able to leave them undisturbed for 2-3 years. Rockery tulips are generally left in the ground

Many bulbs require a period of dry and cool storage when they are dormant. The usual procedure is to lift the bulbs carefully and then allow them to dry for about a week. Discard damaged ones and remove soil. Bulbs with a protective cover (tunic) are stored in boxes or open mesh bags — naked bulbs are stored in boxes of peat or sand

Time of planting is important. With daffodils and other narcissi this is quite early — August to October is the recommended time. This is too early for tulips as early planting can result in frost damage to the shoot tips — November and December are the recommended months

Once flowering is over it is essential to let the foliage die down naturally before removing it — this will ensure that the bulbs regain their size for next year. With daffodils leave the foliage for 6 weeks after flowering — do not tie the leaves into knots

BEGINNING FROM SCRATCH

The first step is to buy good bulbs. With the popular bulbs 'big is best' is a good general rule, but with hyacinths buy bedding-sized and not top-sized bulbs. Buy early to ensure the widest selection and to make sure that the bulbs you buy have not been damaged by constant handling. Avoid ones which are soft, diseased or shrivelled — neither long shoots nor roots should be present.

CONTAINERS

Pots filled with bulbs are a popular way of adding colour, and half of the bulbs we buy are used in this way. They are not ideal as container plants — the flowering period is shorter than that of the average bedding plant and the non-decorative period is long. In addition, bulbs in containers rarely produce a worthwhile second year's display.

Add soilless potting compost to the container and press down gently with your hands — stop when the correct planting level is reached. Add more compost after the bulbs are in place and leave a 3-5 cm watering space at the top of the container. Keep the compost moist.

Layer planting is illustrated above — two or more types with different flowering seasons are planted in layers to extend the display time.

GRASSLAND

'Naturalising' means growing bulbs in grassland or woodland in a way that makes them look like wild flowers. Several bulbs including daffodils, fritillarias and bluebells can be used to enliven a semi-wild area at the back of the lawn.

There are two golden rules. A geometric pattern must be avoided — the classic technique is to drop a handful of bulbs and then plant them where they fall. The tips of small bulbs should be about 5 cm below the surface and larger ones about 10 cm deep. Use a bulb planter if a large area is involved — for a small patch use the technique shown above. The second rule is that it is essential to wait at least 6 weeks after the flowers of spring-flowering types have faded before cutting the grass.

BEDS & BORDERS

(6) Bulbs leave no above-ground indication of their presence after planting. It is therefore sometimes necessary to put in a label to remind you that there are bulbs below

(3) It is vital that there should not be an air space between the bottom of the bulb and the soil at the base of the hole. If the soil is heavy it is useful to put in a shallow layer of grit or moist peat

(4) Push the bulb down to the base of the hole and twist gently. Make sure the bulb is the right way up

(5) Put the earth back and press it down gently. Use the dug-out soil for this job, but it is a good idea to mix it with peat, coarse sand, well-rotted compost or leaf mould if the ground is heavy. Water in if the weather is dry

(2) The width of the hole should be about twice the diameter of the bulb. As a general rule, the common large bulbs such as tulip, narcissus and hyacinth will need to be covered by twice their own height — most small bulbs are covered to about their own height. The bottom should be reasonably flat and the sides reasonably vertical

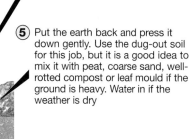

(1) Nearly all bulbs require free-draining soil. Dig about a week before the planting date if the soil is compacted — adding coarse sand or grit will help if the ground is heavy

THE FLOWER-SHY BULB

Flower stems are very few or are missing altogether. Leaves may be absent, unsightly or apparently quite normal. The possible causes are many and varied

• No leaves or flowers

The bulbs may have disappeared — the likely culprits are squirrels or mice and there is nothing you can do. You may find that the bulb is still there but it may have rotted in the soil because of waterlogging during winter. If your soil is heavy remember to improve drainage before planting bulbs next year. Follow the rules on page 27 but decrease the recommended planting depth.

• Leaves weak, discoloured and/or distorted

Several pests and diseases can result in poor foliage and few or no flowers. The most likely culprits are narcissus fly and stem and bulb eelworm — see The Bulb Expert for help in identification. Vine weevil can be a serious pest of container-grown bulbs. Always buy sound, undamaged bulbs. The trouble may be cultural — an unusually late frost or growing a tender variety on a cold site.

• Normal leaves with no flowers or withered buds

One possibility is impatience — some bulbs such as belladonna lily may not flower in the first season, even if top size bulbs are planted. Another cause is the storage of bulbs at too high a temperature, or the effect of an abnormally late frost on tender varieties. The most likely reason for blindness in bulbs (known as grassiness in daffodils and other narcissi) is the use of planting material which is below flowering size. The first step is to make sure you buy top size bulbs, or be prepared to wait a season or more for flowering if you buy or use stored offsets for naturalising. Undersized bulbs will result if you forget to leave at least six weeks between the time when the flowers fade and when you start cutting the foliage or mowing the lawn with naturalised bulbs. Another common cause of grassiness with established daffodils is overcrowding — the answer is to lift and divide the large clumps as described below.

Increasing your stock

Some bulbs spread steadily over the years, and the easiest method of producing extra stock is to lift the clump, divide it and then replant at the appropriate time. True bulbs (narcissi, hyacinths, tulips etc) and corms such as crocuses often form offsets around them and these can be removed for planting. Large offsets from daffodils may flower in the season after planting, but other bulb and corm offsets may take up to 3 years to reach flowering size.

Daffodils can be lifted and divided every 4-5 years to provide more plants or they may have to be divided if over-crowding is causing blindness — see above. Lift and divide in July or August and replant immediately.

The rules are different for snowdrops. Divide large clumps after flowering but while the foliage is still green — replant immediately.

FRUIT TREES

THE NEGLECTED TREE

The bark may be crusty, cracked and cankered. A mass of branches form a criss-crossed jungle of wood and leaves. The fruit is undersized and often pest-ridden

This is a common problem when moving house — the new owner is confronted by a few old apple trees which have obviously been neglected for many years. The first question you must ask yourself is whether the trees are worth saving. It will take several seasons to restore both shape and productivity, and hard work is involved. Don't even think about saving a tree if it is badly cankered. The next question is whether you have the necessary skill — if not, call in a tree surgeon if the tree is 5 or more metres high.

4 STEPS TO FRUIT TREE RENEWAL

STEP 1 Consider spacing. Removal of one or more of the trees will be necessary if they are overcrowded, but this can create a problem. With nearly all apples and pears a pollination partner is needed — a different variety which flowers at approximately the same time and enables cross-pollination to take place. The danger is that removed trees may have been the pollinating partners of the retained specimens. Obviously, don't remove more trees than you have to.

STEP 3 Continue de-horning for the next 2 seasons. This is the term for the cutting back of stout and oversized branches. In addition you should cut out overcrowded secondary branches so as to produce an open-centred tree with its main branches spaced about 60 cm apart. Make sure when cutting back a branch that the piece remaining is large and strong enough to support worthwhile growth in future.

STEP 2 Carry out first-stage surgery. Start to open up and reduce the size of each overgrown tree — this work should take place in winter when the trees are dormant (apples and pears) or shortly after cropping (cherries and plums). It will be necessary to cut out some wood at this time for 3 years — to do all the surgery in a single season would seriously shock the plant. First, remove all dead, diseased and broken branches, and then remove some of the branches which are crossing over others. Finally cut out some of the upright over-tall branches in the heart of the tree.

STEP 4 Feed and mulch each season. The effect of neglect may be that yields will still be disappointing after the renewal programme. It is good practice to feed (a sprinkling of a compound fertilizer worked into the soil around the trunk in spring) and mulch (a layer of compost or well-rotted manure around the trunk in April). If yields remain disappointing, look at the various possible causes listed on page 30.

THE UNPRODUCTIVE TREE

Fruit crop is poor or absent. Blossom may have appeared or it may have been absent — young fruits may have formed and then fallen. Some causes are easy to overcome, but a few are incurable

An apple or pear tree looks attractive when in full blossom in spring, but its primary job in the garden is to produce fruit for the kitchen. Unfortunately there are many reasons why a tree may fail to produce fruit properly — the most likely causes are listed below. Narrow down the cause in your garden by thinking back over past years. Is this the first time that yields have been disappointing, or does it happen every year or every other year?

WHY TREES FAIL TO FRUIT PROPERLY

• No pollination partner
A fine show of blossom every year which then fails to set fruit is generally caused by the absence of a pollination partner nearby. Plant a suitable variety — see The Fruit Expert for recommendations.

• Poor pruning or Careless picking
Over-vigorous pruning of a mature tree will result in abundant growth in the following season, and this will be at the expense of fruiting. Another mistake is cutting back lateral branches from a variety which bears its fruit on the shoot tips. Pulling unripe fruit off the spurs can cause damage and so limit next year's crop.

• Poor spring weather
The effect of a severe frost on open blossom can greatly reduce the crop — this is more likely to occur with pears rather than apples. Very dry air can result in poor pollination, and a wet, cold spring reduces the activity of pollinating insects.

• Overcropping
An apple tree can only support a limited number of large and well-shaped fruit. A heavy crop on the tree after the natural June drop should be thinned or the resulting fruit will be small and next year's crop will be light. Use scissors to remove small and damaged fruits to leave 2 apples per truss.

• Biennial bearing
Some varieties have a tendency to crop heavily one season and then very lightly 12 months later. If biennial cropping is a problem, rub away about half of the fruit buds from the spurs in spring before the expected heavy-cropping season.

• Impatience
You will not obtain high yields from an apple or pear tree until it is 5-7 years old.

• Pests and diseases
Apple troubles which can reduce yield include canker, brown rot and birds. Blossom wilt is a serious disease of plums.

• Poor location or Poor planting
Waterlogging and poor soil result in disappointing yields. There is little you can do with an established tree — the problem should have been tackled at the start. Other poor areas are exposed sites, hilly locations and sunless spots.

• Overvigorous growth
Lush leaf and stem growth with little or no blossom can be caused by feeding too much nitrogen or by pruning too severely. A high-potash fertilizer might help or you can try growing grass around but not up to the tree.

BEGINNING FROM SCRATCH

Plant container-grown plants at any time when the soil is neither frozen nor waterlogged. Planting bare-rooted trees takes place between early November and late March — November is the preferred time

Fifty years is the normal productive life span for an apple tree, but a pear should last for a century or more. You may plan to get rid of a worn-out tree and plant another one, but you should avoid replacing an old apple with another apple, a plum with another plum etc.

Buy a 2 - 4 year old plant from a reputable supplier. Always check the type of rootstock when buying an apple tree. M26 is a good choice for average conditions — it produces a tree which should reach 3 - 4 m. M27 and M9 will produce dwarf bushes reaching no more than 2 - 3 m high, but these dwarfing rootstocks need fertile soil and good growing conditions.

Planting new trees

If you have room for only one apple tree it is a good idea to choose a family tree. Here two to four different but compatible varieties are grafted on to one tree to ensure cross-pollination and a prolonged cropping period.

Follow the planting rules set out on pages 48-49. Before putting in the tree the soil should have been limed if it is very acid and some form of windbreak should have been created if the site is exposed.

Standard trees should be set 10 m apart — leave 5 m between bush types. Remember to plant to the old soil mark — the union with the rootstock should be about 10 cm above ground level.

Stake container-grown trees as shown — for the way to stake bare-rooted plants see page 50.

Pruning established trees

Winter is the time to prune apples and pears.

Spur-bearing variety: Remove dead and badly-diseased wood. Cut back crossing branches and any vigorous laterals crowding into the centre. Leave leaders alone inside the head, but cut back each lateral which is growing beyond the branch leader. With growth outside the head leave both leaders and laterals alone.

Overcrowded, undersized fruit may become a problem. If this happens, thin some of the fruiting spurs and cut out some laterals.

Tip-bearing variety: Remove dead, diseased and overcrowded wood. Then cut back some leaders, but leave alone all laterals which have fruit buds at their tips.

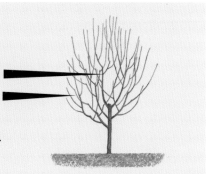

SOFT FRUIT

THE UNPRODUCTIVE PLANT

Fruit crop is poor or absent. There are many causes but two overshadow all the others — birds and viruses. Do not replace a poor-performing plant with one of the same type

Soft fruit needs attention — regular pruning and pest control are necessary. But even with skilled care you will need to replace the plants after a time. Strawberries should remain productive for 3 - 4 years and bush or cane fruit (raspberries, gooseberries etc) for 10 - 12 years.

WHY PLANTS FAIL TO FRUIT PROPERLY

• Impatience
Strawberries and melons will fruit in the first season, but other types take time before providing a full crop. Raspberries — 3 years. Gooseberries, blackcurrants, red currants — 4 years.

• Poor location or Poor planting
Too much shade, poor soil, poor drainage, cold winds and planting at the wrong depth can all lead to disappointing yields.

• Pests and diseases
A large number of insects, fungi and bacteria can affect leaves, stems and fruits. Viruses are especially important and infected plants get steadily worse as time passes. There are a number of soil-borne problems, including honey fungus, strawberry red core (grow a resistant variety) and strawberry verticillium wilt (grow a resistant variety).

• Water and food shortage
Soft fruit plants are often shallow rooting — regular and thorough watering is usually necessary during dry weather. Potash shortage is a cause of poor yields.

• Frost
A serious problem of soft fruit. Cover strawberry plants with cloches, newspaper or horticultural fleece if frost is forecast at blossom time.

• Poor pruning or Careless picking
There are no general pruning rules — look at a guide such as The Fruit Expert if you don't know how. Careless picking can be a problem. Tugging unripe fruit away from the stem can break fruiting spurs and damage stems. The remaining fruit may not ripen.

• Birds
In nearly every case you can expect birds to reduce or eliminate a ripening crop. Netting is the only answer.

• Poor pollination
Rain, cold weather, strong winds and very dry air can all lead to defective pollination.

• Old age
Soft fruit has a limited life span in the garden — see the introduction above.

TREES & SHRUBS

Trees and shrubs are usually the major problem area in the overgrown or neglected garden. Can I simply cut back all the tips of branches growing into a neighbouring bush? Wait — this may result in even more branches developing near the cut ends and so matters will get even worse. Should I then cut all the main branches back and leave the trunk or main stem to produce new ones? Wait — this can be fatal with some trees. Then do I just dig out or cut down some of the trees or shrubs in the crowded group? Wait — this may give rise to one of the problems described below. There are times when one of these tasks is appropriate, and it is the main purpose of this section to help you choose the right procedure for your situation.

BEFORE YOU START

Armed with loppers, secateurs etc you have decided to work on a tree or large shrub. It may be the right thing to do, but equally it might be a job to avoid. There are questions to answer before you start

There is no problem if you plan to carry out the routine pruning which is required each year, provided that you know what to do. The problem arises if you plan to remove the tree or shrub, or carry out major surgery. Think very carefully as this drastic action may have an unwanted effect. With a dead tree the answer is simple — it has to go. But with a living tree the position is not straightforward. Removal can reveal an ugly view which was previously hidden or it may take support away from neighbouring plants. You must be careful when removing a large tree growing close to the house — see page 47. Major tree surgery can also create problems — some trees and shrubs cannot tolerate drastic pruning. If you do plan to go ahead, check that the tree is not protected by a Tree Preservation Order (TPO) — see page 35. Having crossed that hurdle you must decide on who should do the work. Employ a tree surgeon if you do not have the strength and skill required.

WHAT THE WORDS MEAN

Shrub

A shrub is a perennial plant which bears several woody stems at ground level. A mature shrub may be only a few centimetres high or as tall as 6 m, depending on variety. You can expect to have flowers during every month of the year by planting quite a modest selection. Bought primarily to provide attractive foliage and/or flowers — the shape is often of secondary importance.

Framework Shrub: 2 m or over — use as a focal point or with others to provide the framework of the shrub or mixed border.

Fill-in Shrub: 50 cm - 2 m — most shrubs belong here. In a small garden use as framework plants — in a large garden they can be used as ground cover under trees and large shrubs.

Ground-cover Shrub: under 50 cm — wide-spreading and low-growing. Use as a weed-smothering blanket for covering bare ground.

Several shrubs, such as Pyracantha, winter jasmine and Kerria, are not true climbers but are commonly grown against walls and trellis-work.

The dividing line between trees and shrubs is not always clear-cut. Several shrubs, such as holly, dogwood and hazel may grow as small trees.

Climber

A climber is a perennial plant which has the ability to attach itself to or twine around an upright structure. This climbing habit may not develop until the plant is well-established.

Tree

A tree is a perennial woody plant with a clearly-defined trunk or main stem. A mature tree may be only 60 cm high or as tall as 30 m or more, depending on variety.

Conifer

A conifer is a perennial plant which bears cones. These cones are nearly always made up of scales, but there are exceptions (e.g yew). The leaves are usually evergreen but there are exceptions (e.g larch). A mature conifer may be only 30 cm high or as tall as 30 m or more, depending on variety. A popular group bought primarily for their architectural shape.

Hedge

A formal hedge is a continuous line of shrubs, trees or conifers in which the individuality of each plant is lost. An informal hedge is a line of shrubs, trees or conifers in which some or all of the natural outline of the plant is preserved. It is usual to plant just one variety, but this is not essential. The traditional hedge is formal and may need to be clipped regularly in summer — see page 51. A flowering hedge is informal and is cut when the flowers fade.

Deciduous
A plant which loses its leaves at the end of the growing season.

Evergreen
A plant which retains its leaves in a living state during the winter.

Semi-evergreen
A plant which keeps its leaves in a mild winter but loses some or all of its foliage in a hard one.

Lateral branch
A side branch which arises from a main stem.

Head
The framework of stems borne at the top of the stem of a standard.

Spur
A short leaf-bearing shoot which does not increase in size.

Leader
A main shoot on which laterals are produced.

Standard
A tree or trained shrub with a 2 m tall branch-free main stem. A half-standard has a 1 m stem.

THE
DEAD TREE
or SHRUB

Make removal of dead trees and large shrubs a priority job. They give the garden a run-down look and a tall dead tree is a hazard

Before cutting down a tree it will be necessary to find out from your local council planning department if there is a Tree Preservation Order in operation. There is no legal requirement to inform your neighbour, but a word prior to any major tree work can prevent future arguments.

Trees taller than 5 m usually require a tree surgeon, who will be responsible for disposing of the timber and stump. If you have tackled the job yourself it will be necessary to get rid of the wood. Burning on a bonfire is the usual way, but converting some or all into mulching material with a shredder should be considered.

WHY TREES & SHRUBS DIE

• Old age
Some trees like oaks and yews can live for hundreds of years, but there are a few shrubs such as broom which may die after a few years for no apparent reason.

• Poor site preparation
A shrub or tree growing in poorly-drained soil is likely to succumb to root-rotting diseases.

• Fatal diseases
Die-back, silver leaf, fireblight, clematis wilt, honey fungus, dutch elm, canker and butt rot can all kill susceptible plants.

• Wind rock
A serious problem on exposed sites. Staking of tall specimens until they are fully established is essential in these locations.

• Winter damage and Spring scorch
An abnormally severe winter can cause heavy losses, especially if the plants are evergreen and rather tender. Bright sunny weather after a cold spell can lead to the death of evergreens.

• Poor planting material
There are two serious conditions to watch for. Large girdling roots may wrap around the soil ball if the plant has been in the container for a prolonged period — this inhibits further root development. Another situation which can lead to early death is the drying out of the root system before planting.

• Poor planting
Failure to water in thoroughly, allowing the soil ball to break, and planting without firming the compost around the roots can all lead to early death.

• Water shortage
It is vital to make sure that trees and shrubs are watered in prolonged dry weather during the first season in the garden.

• Poor choice
Growing a sun lover in shade or an acid lover in chalky soil is a recipe for failure.

• Rabbits and Deer
These animals can cause havoc with young stock in rural areas — tree guards are the answer.

PRUNING

Renewal pruning is the basic technique for restoring overgrown trees and shrubs. There are some general rules (page 40) but plants have their own requirements — read the A - Z guide (pages 41 - 46) before you begin

It is generally necessary to carry out routine pruning (page 38) every year on most shrubs and some trees. There are three reasons for this task. Firstly, there is the need to remove poor quality wood, such as weak twigs, dead or diseased branches and damaged stems. Next, there is the need to shape the tree or bush — this calls for the removal of good quality but unwanted wood so that the vigour of the plant is directed as required. Finally, trees and shrubs are pruned to regulate the quality and quantity of flower production. The craft of pruning is perhaps the most difficult job the gardener has to learn. Both the timing and the technique depend on the age and type of tree or shrub.

Renewal pruning (page 39) differs in two ways. In order to rejuvenate the tree or shrub the amount of wood is usually greater, and the work often extends over two or more years to ensure that the plant is not seriously checked or killed.

PRUNING TOOLS

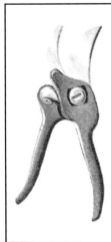

The most important tool is a pair of **secateurs**. Make sure before buying that they are the right size for your hand and invest in a good pair. Both the curved blade types and the anvil ones have their disciples — the important thing is to keep the blade or blades clean and sharp. The maximum cutting diameter is 12 mm (living stems) and 8 mm (dead stems).

For larger shoots use a **straight pruning saw** or a **grecian curved saw** — ordinary carpentry saws tend to jam when used to cut live branches. Alternatively you can use **loppers** for stems 12 - 40 mm across — quicker than a saw. **Extendable long-handled pruners** will enable you to reach high branches without having to use a ladder. A cord-operated **tree lopper** will enable you to reach even greater heights.

A **pruning knife** is useful for cleaning up ragged pruning cuts — professional gardeners use one for cutting back small branches, but this technique is best left to them. A stout pair of **gloves** is essential if you plan to work on prickly shrubs. Depending on the size of your hedge choose a pair of **garden shears** or an **electric hedge trimmer**.

PRUNING METHODS

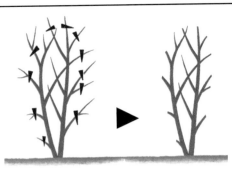

Heading back
The ends of the branches are removed

This may be the removal of just tips or practically all the stems (coppicing or pollarding — see page 39). The immediate effect is to produce a shrub which is smaller than before. But the buds below the cut are then stimulated and will burst into growth so the long-term effect is to produce a tree or shrub which is bushier and leafier than one left unpruned

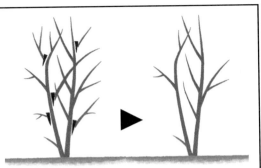

Thinning
Entire branches are cut right back to the main stem

This may be the removal of just one or two branches or the removal of all the branches from the main stem below the crown to produce a standard tree. The immediate effect is to direct extra energy to the remaining branches. Their growth will be accelerated, so the long-term effect is to produce a tree or shrub which is bigger and more open than one left unpruned

Shearing

All the growing points with only a small amount of stem attached are removed by cutting with shears or a hedge trimmer. This technique is used to maintain the shape of hedges and topiary

Pinching

The growing points with only a small amount of stem attached are removed one at a time by nipping out with your fingernails. This technique is used to make small plants bushier

Lopping
The removal of a large branch from the trunk of a tree

Make a smooth sloping cut beyond the raised ridge (branch collar) at the base of the branch — leaving the collar on the tree will speed up healing. Begin by making a shallow cut on the underside, then saw downwards to sever the branch. Consider using a tree surgeon if the branch is heavy or out of reach

In-season pruning

It is not practical to remove the dead flowers from most trees and shrubs, but there are a few large-flowering varieties which benefit from **dead-heading**. Cut the spent flowers after lilac has bloomed — once the flowers of rhododendrons have faded carefully break off the dead blooms without damaging the buds below. Do not remove the dead flower-heads of mophead hydrangeas until March. **Reversion pruning** is essential for variegated trees and shrubs. These plants sometimes produce all-green shoots which are more vigorous than the variegated ones — these should be cut right back to the main stem as soon as they are seen

ROUTINE PRUNING

As a general rule most trees and shrubs grown for their foliage require little regular pruning — all that is necessary is the removal of dead and badly damaged wood together with the pruning back of over-long branches. Flowering shrubs are different — some will soon become leggy and unproductive if not cut back regularly. Do not guess what to do — some shrubs are damaged by hard pruning. Follow the rules below, but if in doubt remember that too little pruning is safer than too much.

STEP 1

Pick the right time. It is essential that pruning takes place at the correct growth stage of the tree or shrub — cutting back severely at the wrong time often leads to the loss of a whole season's flowers and occasionally it leads to the death of the plant.

The best plan is to look up the particular tree or shrub in the A - Z guide — the following timing rules are only a general guide and there are exceptions.

Foliage deciduous trees & shrubs	Between January and March
Deciduous trees & shrubs which bloom before the end of May	As soon as flowering has finished — do not delay
Deciduous trees & shrubs which bloom after the end of May	Between January and March — do not wait until growth starts
Flowering cherries	Late summer
Broad-leaved evergreens	May
Conifers	Autumn

STEP 2

Cut out dead wood. It is quite natural for the lower branches of some shrubs and trees to die under the dense canopy of the upper leaves. Prune back to where the dead branch joins the stem from which it arose.

STEP 3

Cut out damaged and diseased wood. All branches which have been broken by wind or snow should be removed and all badly diseased or cankered wood should be cut out. The pruned surface should not bear tell-tale brown staining.

STEP 4

Cut out weak and overcrowded wood. Prune all very thin and weak stems — then stand back and look at the network of branches. If there is a tightly-packed arrangement of criss-crossed stems at the centre of the bush, some thinning of the old wood will help to open up the shrub and improve its vigour and appearance.

STEP 5

Remove suckers. With grafted plants the suckering growth produced from the rootstock will weaken the plant and may allow these unwanted stems to take over if left unchecked. Some shrubs which grow on their own roots may also produce suckers, and these too should be removed if you want to keep the plant within bounds. Failure to remove the suckers can lead to a dense thicket of stems within a few years.

STEP 6

Cut back overgrowth. Once again stand back and look at the plant. Are some of the branches awkwardly placed? Is it becoming too invasive? Are the stems overhanging the path? Remember that overgrowth should be tackled every year and not left until major surgery is required.

STEP 7

Prune (if necessary) for floral display. Many but not all flowering shrubs and trees require pruning each year to ensure a regular and abundant supply of flowering stems. Look up the plant in the A - Z guide — the following rules are only a general guide and there are exceptions:

Deciduous trees and shrubs which bloom before the end of May. Examples: Ribes, Forsythia, Philadelphus, winter-flowering jasmine, Weigela and Deutzia	Flowers are produced on old wood. Cut back the branches which have flowered — remove about one third of the length. With vigorous shrubs a few of the oldest stems can be cut down to ground level. New, vigorous growth will develop and this will bear flowers next season.
Deciduous trees and shrubs which bloom after the end of May. Examples: Fuchsia, Potentilla, Tamarix, Buddleia davidii	Flowers are produced on new wood. The old stems should be cut back — the amount of wood to remove depends on the tree or shrub concerned. New, vigorous growth will develop and this will bear flowers this season.
Flowering cherries	No further pruning needed.

RENEWAL PRUNING

Renewal pruning involves the removal of more wood than is generally recommended for routine annual pruning. There are several reasons why you may wish to carry out this type of pruning on a tree or shrub. It may be that the plant gives the appearance of being worn out — lanky stems with a poor display of foliage, misshapen branches, disappointing blossom and so on. Renewal pruning should help to rejuvenate it, but remember that it may be necessary to extend the work over two or more seasons to avoid killing the plant by too-drastic surgery. Also remember that not all over-age shrubs are worth saving. Another reason for renewal pruning is that the tree or shrub is growing too vigorously. It may be too tall, it may be casting too much shade or it may be growing into adjoining plants, walls etc. On the other hand it may be growing too slowly and has lost its bushiness — it may be worth trying renewal pruning before deciding to get rid of it. Some of the pruning methods on page 37 are used in renewal pruning, but there are additional techniques which are illustrated below.

Crown lifting
Lower branches are removed by lopping (page 37)

This technique lets in more light and allows freer access under the tree, but it should be used with care on trees with a weeping growth habit

Pollarding
All branches are removed from the top of the trunk by lopping (page 37)

This technique is used to keep large trees under control or to ensure the production of a head of attractive young stems. Not all trees can be pollarded — see A - Z guide for suitable ones

Crown reducing
Side and upper branches are shortened by heading back (page 37)

This technique brings tree or shrub growth under control — both height and spread are reduced. Take care to maintain the basic shape

Coppicing
All branches are cut back to ground level

This technique is used to replace existing growth with fresh young stems which have colourful bark or attractive foliage. Not all shrubs can be coppiced, but some (see A - Z guide) require this technique for maximum display

RENEWAL PRUNING : STEP-BY-STEP GUIDE

STEP 1	**Check if the tree or shrub needs renewal pruning.** Unless the garden has been neglected for a number of years most of the trees and shrubs will require only routine pruning at the recommended time each year — see page 38. There are some which may require renewal pruning — before you start ask the following questions to make sure that it requires this more drastic treatment. Is it growing too tall or spreading into other plants, over fences, into walls etc? Is it looking old and tired with lots of dead or unproductive wood, leggy branches with few leaves, seriously decreased floral display etc? Is it looking reasonably healthy but growing too slowly with poor leaf growth despite being properly fed and watered?
STEP 2	**Pick the right time.** Winter is the usual time for foliage types — check the A - Z guide for exceptions. Do not prune in frosty weather. You may wish to prune early flowering shrubs after flowering to avoid losing next season's blooms, but wholesale cutting back is easier in winter. Flowering cherries and closely related species should be dealt with in late summer.
STEP 3	**Cut out dead wood.** Even with healthy trees and shrubs you are likely to find some dead branches. These should be pruned back to where the dead wood joins the stem from which it arose. Leaving this job until winter can pose a problem with deciduous plants — it can be difficult to distinguish between dead and living mature branches when there are no leaves. It is a good idea to do this step in early autumn before the leaves fall.
STEP 4	**Cut out damaged and diseased wood.** All branches which have been broken by wind or snow should be removed and all badly diseased and cankered wood should be cut out. The pruned surface should not bear tell-tale brown staining.
STEP 5	**Cut out weak wood and suckers.** Prune all very thin and weak stems. Thin out the oldest branches if there is a tightly-packed arrangement of criss-crossed stems at the centre of a bush. Remove suckers — failure to remove them can lead to a dense thicket of stems.
STEP 6	**Carry out pruning treatment.** At this stage follow the instructions in the A - Z guide for the particular tree or shrub. If a large amount of wood has to be removed it is usually wise to spread the work over two or more seasons. If looking up instructions for each individual shrub seems like too much trouble or if you don't know the name of the plant being pruned then you can try the general renewal pruning technique below. But be warned — some shrubs really do need specialised treatment. 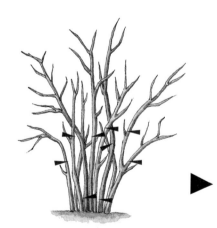 Cut back about one stem in three to approximately 10 cm above ground level — choose the oldest and woodiest stems first. Then cut back the remaining stems to about half their height. Repeat this treatment next year.
STEP 7	**Provide post-pruning treatment.** Major surgery is a shock to the plant's system. Help recovery by applying a general fertilizer around the root zone in spring, putting down a mulch in May and watering in dry weather if the root system is shallow or restricted.

RENEWAL PRUNING : A – Z

ACER	Large ash, maple and sycamore trees can be cut back in winter. Types with variegated leaves can be pollarded each year for maximum foliage effect. Japanese maples are susceptible to frost damage — cut back dead stem tips in spring, but avoid hard pruning
AESCULUS	Horse chestnut responds well to crown reducing when growth gets out of hand — crown lifting will be necessary when shade below the branches becomes a problem. Large trees can be hard pruned
AMELANCHIER	To maintain it as a tree rather than as a shrub it is necessary to cut away the suckers at the base and to remove the side-shoots which regularly appear on the trunk. Large trees can be hard pruned
ARUNDINARIA	The bamboos are attractive when young but can soon become a spreading problem. Thin congested clumps by cutting dead and some of the older stems down to ground level in spring
AUCUBA	Hard pruning is not a problem. In spring lop off unwanted large branches as required and cut back other branches to give you the shape you desire. Use secateurs, not shears
BERBERIS	Little or no routine pruning is usually required, but berberis can soon outgrow its allotted space. For renewal pruning carry out step 6 (page 40) in February with deciduous varieties or immediately after flowering with evergreens
BETULA	Mature birches may benefit from moderate crown lifting in summer — spread the work over 2 or more seasons to avoid shocking the tree
BUDDLEIA	If a B. davidii or B. globosa shrub is overgrown then renew it by cutting it down to about 1 m high in March. Carry out routine pruning in subsequent years. The head of B. alternifolia can become a mass of overgrown twisted branches — pollard in late summer and accept losing next year's blooms
BUXUS	Box is not harmed by hard pruning. A bush can be drastically cut back in spring without ill-effect, but to avoid large bare patches extend the work over 2 - 3 seasons
CALLUNA	Trim back lightly in spring to restore the plants — do not cut into old leafless wood. Dig out and replace bushes with bare centres or ones growing in alkaline soil
CAMELLIA	Worn-out leggy plants can be renewed by hard pruning. Remove the oldest branches in spring — cut back the remainder in the following spring
CARYOPTERIS	Cut all the stems back to about 5 cm above ground level in March. Coppice in this way every year
CEANOTHUS	You should rely on routine pruning — it does not respond well to hard pruning. In March cut back flowered shoots of deciduous species to within 10 cm of the previous year's growth. With evergreens take the ends off shoots when they have finished flowering
CERATOSTIGMA	Cut all stems back to about 5 cm above ground level in April. Coppice in this way every year
CERCIS	The judas tree does not respond well to hard pruning — do not remove large living branches
CHAENOMELES	A worn-out japonica can be cut down to ground level in winter — thin out the resulting suckers to create a new framework of stems

Berberis darwinii

Buddleia davidii 'Harlequin'

Camellia japonica 'Tricolor'

Ceanothus 'Autumnal Blue'

CHOISYA	Mexican orange blossom is one of the shrubs which will tolerate hard pruning provided you do the job over 2 or 3 seasons. Cut back the first section of the overgrown bush in April and the next section next year
CISTUS	The sun rose does not respond to renewal pruning — old wood does not produce new shoots. You can cut back over-long and damaged shoots in spring, but old and leggy plants should be replaced
CLEMATIS	The routine pruning of clematis is a complicated business — always keep the label when you plant one of these climbers. An old neglected plant is a tangled mass of stems — and renewal pruning is simple. Cut off the top growth in March at about waist height, leaving the main stem or stems. Feed and water
CONIFERS	Very few conifers (e.g yew) are able to produce new growth on old wood, so renewal pruning is rarely an option. A tree or large shrub which is far too large and vigorous for its allotted space is best removed, but you can try topping it and shaping the outer branches if it is still young and well-clothed with leaves. A wide-spreading branch of a low-growing conifer which is interfering with its neighbour should be cut back to a point under a covering branch. Large brown patches caused by disease or drought are a problem. Cutting them away leaves a bare patch which is unsightly, and this will not fill in with new growth. Removal may be the only answer
CORNUS	The cane-stemmed dogwood with coloured bark should be coppiced (page 39) in March. Treat an overgrown cornelian cherry (C. mas) in the same way
CORYLUS	Coppicing (page 39) is the best renewal technique for hazel — named varieties with coloured leaves or contorted stems should be pollarded (page 39) instead
COTINUS	The smoke bush can be cut back to about 15 cm above ground level, otherwise follow step 6 on page 40
COTONEASTER	Cotoneasters will produce new shoots from old wood after hard pruning, but drastic pruning will change the shape of the bush. An overgrown specimen can be cut back to near ground level in February (deciduous species) or April (evergreens)
CRATAEGUS	Over-long branches can be headed back or lopped off in late winter, but drastic renewal pruning is not recommended for hawthorn
CYTISUS	Brooms do not respond to renewal pruning — old wood does not produce new shoots. You can cut back over-long and damaged shoots in spring, but old and leggy plants should be replaced
DAPHNE	Daphne does not respond to renewal pruning — old wood does not produce new shoots. Cut off dead and damaged shoots and then leave alone, or dig out and replace
DEUTZIA	Carry out step 6 on page 40. Prune this bush regularly once it has been brought back to its former self
ELAEAGNUS	Follow step 6 on page 40 — when cutting back branches in April or May avoid removing wood which is more than a couple of years old
ERICA	Trim back lightly as soon as the flowers have faded to restore the plants — do not cut into old leafless wood. Exception — overgrown tree heaths should be hard pruned in April
ESCALLONIA	Follow step 6 on page 40 — do this work in April or May

Choisya 'Aztec Pearl'

Juniperus media 'Pfitzeriana'

Crataegus oxyacantha 'Rosea Flore Pleno'

Erica carnea 'Springwood White'

EUCALYPTUS	Gum trees can be hard pruned in late spring. To ensure the production of an attractive display of juvenile foliage you should coppice the plant to leave stems about 15 cm above ground level
EUONYMUS	The evergreen varieties of Euonymus such as Emerald 'n Gold can be pruned hard — cut back unwanted growth in March or April. Step 6 on page 40 is a suitable technique. The deciduous forms (spindle trees) will also tolerate hard pruning
EXOCHORDA	Step 6 (page 40) can be used immediately after flowering to restore an overgrown lanky shrub
FAGUS	Unwanted branches can be lopped off close to the trunk in winter — call in a tree surgeon if the beech tree is large
FORSYTHIA	Step 6 (page 40) after flowering will generally rejuvenate an overgrown bush. If the plant is really out of control you may need more drastic action — stiff-stemmed varieties can be coppiced in February
FRAXINUS	Ash is tolerant of hard pruning, so lopping or heading back branches in late winter will not harm the tree
FUCHSIA	Hardy fuchsias should be cut back to nearly ground level in March. In a mild area it can be left to form a spreading bush — this can be cut back very hard if it gets untidy
GARRYA	A wall-trained or free-standing silk tassel bush will readily regrow if it is cut down in late winter, but you will have to wait a few seasons for blooms to reappear
GENISTA	Brooms do not respond to renewal pruning — old wood does not produce new shoots. You can cut back over-long and damaged shoots in spring, but old and leggy plants should be replaced
HAMAMELIS	Witch hazel does not respond well to hard pruning — lop off rather than cut back unwanted branches after flowering. Avoid major surgery if you can
HEBE	Most overgrown and unsightly hebes can be restored by hard pruning as new shoots develop on old wood. The time for this work is May
HEDERA	Ivy can be a decorative cover, but left unpruned it can be a danger to young trees, unsound walls, gutters and wall-hung tiles. Trim back and remove growing tips as required
HELIANTHEMUM	Cut off over-long and damaged shoots with shears in summer to neaten this low-growing bush, but old and leggy plants should be replaced
HIBISCUS	Tackle an overgrown or unsightly shrub by lopping off unwanted branches and by cutting back some of the remaining ones if necessary. Do not carry out major surgery all at once — stagger it over 2 or more seasons
HYDRANGEA	In spring you can improve the bush by cutting out some of the old woody stems to ground level. Repeat the treatment next year
HYPERICUM	Cut down H. calycinum to ground level in March. Foliage varieties should be treated the same way, but large-flowering types such as H. 'Hidcote' should receive the step 6 (page 40) treatment
ILEX	Spring or summer pruning of holly trees and bushes can be as heavy as you like — prune back branches to shape or cut down to ground level to start again
JASMINUM	The time to work on winter jasmine is when flowering is over. Cut out about one in three branches, starting with the oldest, and then cut back all shoots which have flowered

Euonymus japonicus 'Microphyllus Albus'

Forsythia 'Beatrix Farrand'

Garrya elliptica 'James Roof'

Hydrangea macrophylla 'Blue Wave'

KERRIA	A neglected jew's mallow can become a wide-spreading eyesore. After flowering use a spade to cut away excess growth, then follow step 6 on page 40
LABURNUM	The golden rain tree does not respond well to hard pruning. If major surgery is necessary, do the work in summer and spread the work over several seasons
LAURUS	Renewal pruning should not be a problem — in spring cut out all frost damaged wood and with secateurs and/or loppers cut back the branches to the shape you desire
LAVANDULA	Overgrown lavender is a sprawling unattractive plant which will not respond to hard pruning. You can prune most of last year's growth, but do not cut into old wood. In most cases it is better to start again
LAVATERA	A short-lived plant which needs routine pruning every year. With neglected bushes cut down the stems in April to about 20 cm above the ground
LIGUSTRUM	An overgrown privet poses no problems. In spring cut it back as hard as you like — pruning to 10 cm above ground level will do no harm
LONICERA	Vigorous varieties of climbing honeysuckle can quickly form a mass of tangled untidy stems. To restore stems which can be controlled it will be necessary to remove all the intertwined top growth to straight stems — do not prune lower than waist height
MAGNOLIA	Prune in summer if you have to cut back a magnolia tree or shrub — this plant may not respond well to hard pruning as open wounds have low resistance to disease attack
MAHONIA	Dig out some of the underground stems if growth has spread too widely. In spring follow step 6 (page 40) if the bush has been neglected — repeat the treatment in the next 2 seasons
MALUS	Crab apple trees do not require routine pruning every year like their culinary cousins, but renewal pruning is necessary if they have grown too large for the space available. Carry out crown reduction (page 39) in winter — do not be too drastic
PACHYSANDRA	Height is not a problem if neglected but spread may be — some runners may have to be removed. Cut back to about 5 cm in March if growth is slow
PALMS	Only one true palm (Trachycarpus fortunei) is hardy enough to be considered a garden tree — pruning is done by regularly removing the bottom fan-shaped leaves as they die to ensure the lifting of the crown. The false palm Cordyline australis is much more popular — treat as above to enhance the tree-like appearance
PARTHENOCISSUS	Virginia creeper is a self-clinging climber which can rapidly spread above and beyond where you want it to be. It will quite happily put up with being cut back to a low level — do this work in early winter
PHILADELPHUS	Thinning out the stems of mock orange is necessary in order to bring it back into shape. If the plant is too tall follow step 6 (page 40) — do this work immediately after flowering if you don't want to lose next year's flowers
PHORMIUM	New zealand flax has become a popular choice as a focal-point plant in recent years — small enough at the garden centre but quite quickly a head-high forest of leaves in the garden. You can cut away spreading growth with a spade, but there is nothing you can do to reduce the height
PHOTINIA	Shape the bush by cutting back lanky branches in spring. This is not a plant to cut right back if it gets out of hand

Laburnum watereri 'Vossii'

Lonicera periclymenum 'Serotina'

Mahonia aquifolium

Parthenocissus quinquefolia

PIERIS	Pieris can become gaunt and unattractive if it is not happy with the growing conditions. Fortunately it can cope with hard pruning, so cut back over-long branches in May
PLATANUS	Crown lifting (page 39) of plane trees is carried out regularly to show off the beauty of the bark. Hard pruning is no problem and so crown reduction (page 39) can be used to keep growth under control. The trees can be pollarded (page 39) but this is a technique for street rather than garden trees
POLYGONUM	The rampant russian vine should be cut back in winter — take it to a point where next season's growth will fill but not exceed the space allotted to it
POPULUS	Left unpruned a poplar can grow more quickly than almost any other tree, so plant with care. The garden poplars have attractive colourful leaves — for maximum foliage display pollard the tree in January or February
POTENTILLA	Age and inadequate routine pruning can turn your shrub into a mound of old wood with sparse foliage and even fewer flowers. Renew it by cutting back to 10 - 20 cm above the ground in April
PRUNUS	Flowering types (cherry, plum, almond etc) are pruned in late summer. Restore by lopping off unwanted branches rather than cutting back the shoot ends. Spread any major surgery over several seasons. The laurels are different — these can be cut back as hard as you like in late winter
PYRACANTHA	The firethorn can spread rapidly and become a nuisance. Fortunately it will happily regrow after cutting into old wood, so in late winter trim back or cut down as required
QUERCUS	Oak trees can be pruned in winter to lift or reduce the crown (page 39). Make sure that you do not spoil the shape by over-drastic pruning. Spread major surgery over several seasons
RHODODENDRON	Leggy, bare stems can be cut back in March and April. If the whole shrub is in poor condition cut all the growth down to about 20 - 30 cm above the soil. Azaleas need more gentle pruning — trim back but avoid cutting into old wood
RHUS	Lop off overgrown or misplaced branches in February — remove suckers as they appear. If necessary the plant can be cut back to 30 - 40 cm above the ground
RIBES	Follow step 6 (page 40) as soon as flowering is over. Where space for the bush is a problem, flowering currant can be cut down to 10 cm in late winter
ROBINIA	These decorative trees are quite tolerant of hard pruning and can be cut back hard in winter. The yellow-leaved R. pseudoacacia can be pollarded for maximum foliage effect
ROSMARINUS	You can cut back an old rosemary bush to leave the stout stems about 15 - 30 cm high, but regrowth can be unpredictable and it is best to start again
RUBUS	Both the flowering and whitewashed cane species respond well to hard pruning in late autumn or early spring. Coppice (page 39) the decorative-stemmed ones every year
SALIX	All the willows, including the corkscrew and weeping varieties, can be drastically cut back in winter or spring. Both pollarding and coppicing are techniques used on varieties with colourful leaves or decorative stems
SAMBUCUS	Elder trees are quite happy to be cut back to bare trunks or to near ground level in winter

Pieris formosa forrestii
'Wakehurst'

Potentilla 'Abbotswood'

Rhododendron 'Blue Diamond'

Sambucus nigra
'Aureomarginata'

SANTOLINA	Cotton lavender soon forms an untidy bush with leggy branches if it is not pruned regularly. You can cut back the stems of an overgrown plant to about 8 cm, but it is usually better to start again
SENECIO	A badly neglected Senecio is an unattractive plant. Before deciding to dig out, cut it back to 40 cm above the ground in April to induce new shoot production
SKIMMIA	A neat and compact shrub which is well worth saving if it has grown too large for its space. It can be cut back to near ground level in spring
SORBUS	Neither whitebeam nor mountain ash sprout readily from cut branches so heading back should be kept to a minimum. Prune overgrown trees and shrubs by thinning in early spring — see page 37
SPARTIUM	Spanish broom does not form new shoots on old wood. Old leggy specimens are best replaced
SPIRAEA	Use step 6 (page 40) for bringing an overgrown spring-flowering variety under control — with summer-flowering types cut back the stems in early spring to 5 - 10 cm above the ground
SYMPHORICARPOS	Snowberry is a rampant grower which can spread alarmingly if left unpruned. Tackle a problem plant in early spring by using step 6 (page 40) or by cutting right back
SYRINGA	A common feature of neglected gardens is a lilac with a thicket of tall stems with out-of-sight blooms at the top. Fortunately hard pruning will not cause a problem — cut the plant down to 1 - 2 m in winter
TAMARIX	A shrub which needs routine pruning every year. Cut back a neglected specimen in early spring to leave 1 - 2 m high trunks with a head of short main branch stumps
TILIA	Lime trees will tolerate quite drastic crown lifting and crown reduction — late summer is the best time for this work. Large trees are sometimes pollarded
ULEX	Gorse can be cut back after flowering to restore its shape, but it will not produce new growth on cut old stems. With a vigorous old bush you can cut off the top growth in March to promote new shoots from the rootstock
ULMUS	You can do nothing to restore an elm infected with dutch elm disease — badly infected trees must be removed and burnt. There are resistant species — these should be pruned to shape in winter
VIBURNUM	There is a wide range of Viburnum varieties and these generally receive little routine pruning every year. Old overgrown ones can usually be cut back quite safely in spring to bring them back to shape
VITIS	The wall-covering decorative vines can be cut back in winter if growth is too vigorous
WEIGELA	Renewal pruning is not a problem — follow step 6 (page 40) in summer or cut the whole shrub back in autumn
WISTERIA	The main job with a neglected Wisteria is to make sure that it is properly secured to the wires or supports. Remove some or all of the forward growing old branches and tie in younger growth. Do this in winter — in July cut back the side shoots to about 15 cm
YUCCA	The stemless varieties do not require renewal pruning, although it may be necessary to cut away some of the suckers if the clump starts to spread too widely. Remove old and dead leaves from trunk-forming types to enhance the tree effect

Santolina pinnata 'Neapolitana'

Skimmia japonica 'Rubella'

Viburnum davidii

Wisteria floribunda 'Macrobotrys'

THE UNWANTED TREE or SHRUB

The lowly Exochorda and Lonicera nitida are being engulfed by the Ilex and Rhamnus — obviously they have to go. But the attractively variegated Rhamnus is being deformed by the aggressive Ilex, so regular cutting back is necessary if both are to stay

There are several reasons why you may decide to get rid of a tree or shrub. Perhaps the most usual reason is overcrowding — the inevitable result of planting too closely. Keep the key trees and/or shrubs and get rid of the others, but the decision is often very difficult. Deal with the trees as described on page 35. Shrub removal is usually a do-it-yourself job, but watch your back when pulling out the plant. Another reason for disposal is that the plant is an eyesore or is not growing properly, but think about renewal pruning (pages 39 - 46) before deciding to get rid of a tree or shrub. Growing a flowering climber such as clematis up a misshapen tree can sometimes create an attractive feature at flowering time, but this does not appeal to everyone. A third reason for wanting to remove a tree is a fear that it may damage the house — see below.

Trees and subsidence

Tree roots close to the foundations of a house can cause subsidence during a prolonged drought. The situation is most likely to occur in clayey soil areas. The uptake of water by the roots hastens soil shrinkage, the foundations crack and this results in cracks along the house wall. Listed below are the safe minimum distances between various trees and a house wall. Obviously the best plan is to meet this requirement at planting time, but you may already have a tall tree very close to the house. It is tempting to cut it down straight away, but take care. It may be covered by a Tree Preservation Order, and it is unwise to think of instant removal. This could result in heave, the opposite of subsidence and just as damaging. This is caused by an excess of water in the soil which used to be taken up by the tree roots. The answer is to bring the tree under control by cutting back over a number of years.

Safe distance between tree trunk and house wall

5 m	10 m	20 m	30 m	40 m
Holly	Apple, Pear	Ash	Horse Chestnut	Poplar
Laurel	Birch	Beech	Lime	Willow
Yew	Cherry	C. leylandii	Oak	
	Hawthorn	Gum tree		
	Laburnum	Maple		
	Mountain Ash	Plane		
	Pine	Sycamore		

BEGINNING FROM SCRATCH

Note that the planting hole for a bare-rooted shrub is wide and quite shallow. A common mistake is to force the roots into a deep and narrow hole

You will never finish stocking your beds and borders with woody plants as long as you are a gardener. Trees and shrubs die or fail to flourish, there is the plant at the garden centre you simply must have and there are newly-created plots which must be filled. There is more to planting than digging a hole and dropping in the plant. Doing the right thing may be more complex than you thought, but following the rules will save you from being disappointed later on. Listed below are the things you will need to make sure of success at this initial stage. After planting there are two jobs to do — mulch the area around the newly-planted tree or shrub and water thoroughly during dry spells in late spring or summer, although routine watering should not be necessary once the plant is established.

THE THINGS YOU WILL NEED

HOLE The planting hole for a container-grown plant should be large enough for you to get your hands comfortably down in the space between the soil ball and the sides of the hole. This means that it should be at least 20 cm wider than the diameter of the container. It should be at least 5 cm deeper than the height of the soil ball. With a bare-rooted plant it should be wide enough to allow the roots to be spread out evenly and deep enough to allow the old soil mark on the stem or stems to be at or just below the soil surface.

PLANT Check that the container-grown plant is sturdy and healthy. Judge it by the number of stems and the density of the leaf cover. The presence of flowers and flower buds will tell you that the plant has reached flowering size, but the number of blooms does not necessarily indicate quality. As a general rule it is better to buy a small specimen rather than a large one for instant effect. It will of course be cheaper, but it will also be easier to plant and will establish more rapidly. Remove damaged branches before planting.

PLANTING MIXTURE Unless your soil is a crumbly loam it is advisable to fill the hole with a planting mixture rather than the earth which you have removed from the planting hole. Mix together 1 part soil with 1 part moist peat in a wheelbarrow and store in a shed until required.

TREE GUARD If rabbits and/or deer are a problem it will be necessary to protect the stems of most newly-planted trees. The easiest way is to use a plastic tree guard wound round the trunk. Protecting newly-planted shrubs is more difficult — a tall strip of wire-netting around the whole plant until it is established is effective, but it is unsightly.

STAKE A tree or spindly bush can be rocked by strong winds if its roots are not able to anchor it to the ground. A newly-planted specimen does not have this anchorage, so it can be blown over or dislodged. Staking at planting time is the answer — see page 50.

TIMING

CONTAINER-GROWN PLANTS

JULY	AUG	SEPT	OCT	NOV	DEC	JAN	FEB	MARCH	APRIL	MAY	JUNE

BARE-ROOTED PLANTS &
PRE-PACKAGED PLANTS

Container-grown plants can be planted at any time, but it is advisable to avoid the depths of winter and midsummer. The time for planting bare-rooted and pre-packaged plants is between mid October and late November, but if the weather is wet or if the soil is heavy then it is better to wait until March. The ground should be neither frozen nor waterlogged. Squeeze a handful of soil — it should be wet enough to form a ball and yet dry enough to shatter when dropped on to a hard surface.

PLANTING

Container-grown plant

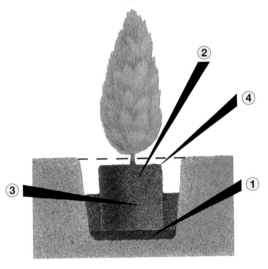

Bare-rooted plant

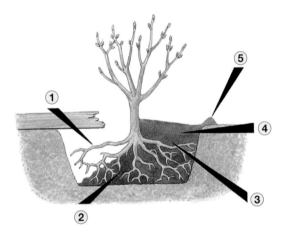

(1) The hole should be wide enough to allow you to firm the planting mixture with your hands — see page 48. It should be deep enough to ensure that the top of the soil ball will be about 3 cm below the soil surface after planting. Put a 3 - 5 cm layer of planting mixture (see page 48) in the hole.

(2) The container should have been watered thoroughly at least an hour before planting. Remove the plant carefully from the container and stand the root ball on a piece of plastic sheeting.

(3) Examine the exposed surface. Pull out or cut away any encircling roots and gently tease out some of the roots on the surface. Gently place the plant in the hole. Slowly fill the space between the soil ball and the sides of the hole with planting mixture — press down each layer with your hands.

(4) Tread down gently once the space is full — do not stamp down. Add more planting mixture if necessary, but you should leave a shallow water-holding basin at the top. Water in thoroughly.

(1) Set a board across the top of the hole — hold the plant against the board and check that the hole is wide enough and deep enough — see page 48. Cut back damaged roots — shorten very long ones to 30 cm.

(2) Work a couple of trowelsful of planting mixture around the roots. Shake the plant gently up and down — add a little more planting mixture and firm around the roots with your fists.

(3) Half-fill the hole with more planting mixture and firm it down by gentle treading. On no account should you stamp heavily. Start treading at the outer edge of the hole and work gradually inwards.

(4) Add more planting mixture until the hole is full. Tread down once again and then loosen the surface. Spread a little soil around the stem so that a low dome is formed.

(5) The final step is to build a low ridge of soil around the edge of the hole when planting is finished. This will form a water retaining basin. Water the plant in by filling this basin.

PLANTING MATERIAL

CONTAINER-GROWN

A container-grown plant may be expensive but it has one great advantage — it can be planted at any time of the year. It is not, however, fool-proof — you have to choose and plant with care. Avoid sickly specimens and use a planting mixture (page 48) for filling the hole.

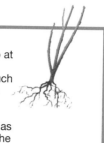

BARE-ROOTED

A bare-rooted plant is dug up at the nursery and the soil is removed — damp material such as peat is packed around the roots. Some shrubs will root more readily than container-grown ones when planted out as bare-rooted stock. Never let the roots dry out.

PRE-PACKAGED

Pre-packaged shrubs are the plants sold by DIY stores and supermarkets. They are bare-rooted plants with roots in peat and packed in a plastic bag. Inexpensive, but you cannot see the condition of the plant and in store conditions premature growth may occur.

OWN GARDEN STOCK

Plants in the wrong place and rooted cuttings have to be moved. Early autumn is the best time for evergreens — late autumn for deciduous plants. Water thoroughly before lifting — keep soil around the roots. Cut back shrub stems to knee-high.

SPACING

The shrubs from the garden centre are usually small — when planted at the recommended distances the spaces in between look bare and unsightly. But the plants will grow, and if you have planted too closely there are only two alternatives. You can either dig out some of the cramped shrubs (which is the more sensible but less popular choice) or you can hack them back each year which takes time and can also destroy much of their beauty. The right thing is to follow the guide below.

Recommended planting distance for most shrubs and trees

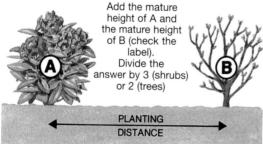

Add the mature height of A and the mature height of B (check the label). Divide the answer by 3 (shrubs) or 2 (trees)

PLANTING DISTANCE

Use the rule of thumb guide below if you do not know the expected mature height of the plants:

Trees — 5 - 8 m apart, depending on whether they are small, medium or large types

Shrubs — 0.5 m - 1.5 m apart, depending on whether they are small, medium or large types

Do not plant trees close to water pipes, drains etc.

STAKING

Plants which may be dislodged by the wind require staking at the time of planting. Buy a stake which has been treated with a preservative — place it on the side from which the prevailing wind blows. Follow the instructions below for a bare-rooted plant. For a container-grown tree a variation of this technique is required — see page 31.

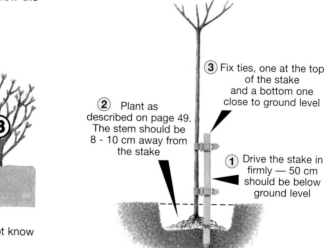

③ Fix ties, one at the top of the stake and a bottom one close to ground level

② Plant as described on page 49. The stem should be 8 - 10 cm away from the stake

① Drive the stake in firmly — 50 cm should be below ground level

Leave the ties loose at first and then tighten after a few weeks when the tree has settled. Adjust the ties once or twice a year as the stem thickens. Remove the stake after 3 years.

THE NEGLECTED HEDGE

An overgrown and gappy hedge tells everyone that the garden has been neglected. It is vital to restore the hedge, but before you begin it is necessary to learn the right way to tackle the job

There are two basic types. The traditional or formal hedge is a line of shrubs or trees in which the individuality of each plant is lost. It is grown for its leafiness and is clipped once or more during the growing season to maintain its smooth appearance. Examples include yew, privet, beech, cypress and laurel. The informal hedge is different. It is a line of shrubs or trees where some or all of the natural outline of the plant is preserved. Most are flowering and/or berrying types (e.g rose, pyracantha, escallonia and lavender) and here pruning is timed to ensure a decorative display.

Restoring a formal hedge

The popular quartet (yew, privet, box and laurel) can all be drastically cut back into old wood without coming to any harm. At the other end of the scale the conifers (except yew) will not sprout from pruned old wood.

The standard plan is to cut back one face of the hedge this season and then prune the other face next year. A flat top is acceptable if it is narrow — wide-topped hedges should be tapered so as to avoid snow damage.

The best time to prune is late winter for deciduous types and spring for evergreens. Feed and mulch in mid spring and water during dry weather. Gaps in the hedge can be filled in. Buy small plants — never try to match the height of the existing ones.

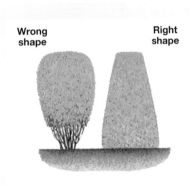

Wrong shape **Right shape**

Starting from scratch

The first task is to decide the planting line. This needs some thought — right next to the pavement might seem a good idea, but there could be a serious overhang problem in years to come. Having decided on the line, dig out a 1 m wide strip. This trench should be 50 cm deep — put a layer of well-rotted manure or compost at the bottom. Single-row planting is acceptable if economy is necessary and quick screening is not, but double-row planting is recommended. Plant out, using page 49 for guidance. After planting stretch wires tightly along the young plants and attach them to it with ties. Keep the plants watered during dry weather.

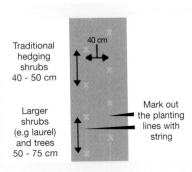

Traditional hedging shrubs 40 - 50 cm

40 cm

Larger shrubs (e.g laurel) and trees 50 - 75 cm

Mark out the planting lines with string

PONDS

A pond should be a thing of beauty which provides interest all year round, but it will steadily deteriorate if it was not constructed on a suitable site and has not been properly maintained. The major problems are listed in this section — most take time and effort to solve.

THE GREEN POND

Algae are the cause of the green colour in your pond. Chemicals may help but the real answer is to create conditions in which these primitive plants will not thrive

There are two types of algae which affect garden ponds. The first type are the microscopic ones which turn the water green. The other type are the blanketweeds — long and silky green threads which are attached to the bottom and sides of the pond. The cause is simple to understand. Sunlight coupled with mineral salts and organic matter in the water greatly stimulate the algae.

Creating the correct pond balance (see below) is the only really satisfactory way of keeping algae at bay but unfortunately this is not always possible. The usual answer is to use a chemical treatment. The growth of algae is worst in the spring — buy an algicide and add it to the water. If fish and/or plants are present it is vital to follow the instructions carefully. Repeat as necessary.

Pond Balance

Each of the components of the pond — water, plant life, soil, fish and dead organic matter must be balanced so that the growth of algae is inhibited.

The first need is to keep down the amount of unwanted organic matter. Remove dead plants and fallen leaves, do not incorporate peat, compost or soluble fertilizers when potting up plants and do not give more food than the fish can eat in a short time. Next, provide some shade. Grow water lilies and/or other plants so that half the surface is covered. The third basic need is to deprive the algae of the carbon dioxide and minerals which are essential for their development. This task is performed by the oxygenators — lowly underwater plants which play a vital role in keeping the water clear. They also supply oxygen which is utilised by the fish. Pond size is a critical factor — even if you do all the recommended things it will still be impossible to achieve proper balance in a pond of less than 4 sq.m.

Your pond will always turn cloudy and slightly green in spring, but with proper balance it will soon clear once active plant growth begins.

THE OVERGROWN POND

Plant aquatics in baskets rather than in the soil at the bottom of the pond. The time will come when water lilies will need lifting and dividing, and having to empty the pond to do this is a tedious task

Just a couple of years ago the pond may have been the envy of your neighbours — neat patches of water lilies with other water plants providing spots of interest within and around the edges of the pool.

Now it is an eyesore. The surface has been taken over by one or two aggressive types and the water lily leaves are crowded and growing well above the water — an extensive mass of leaves with few flowers. Water lilies take 4 - 8 years to reach this stage.

Lifting and dividing is the only answer. Choose a mild day in late spring and start to lift the baskets which house the roots. Divide the plants, selecting pieces with vigorous new growth and a plentiful supply of roots. Throw away the old woody core. Remove any old leaves and wash away the soil — at no stage should the roots be allowed to dry out. Replant in baskets filled with aquatic-plant compost — use new ones if the existing ones are badly distorted. If the water lilies are rooted in the mud at the bottom, you will have to clean out the pond — see below.

Cleaning out a small pond

There are several reasons why it may be necessary to clean out the pond. It may be leaking, the water may be polluted or there may be a thick layer of silt and rotting organic matter at the bottom.

Spring or summer is the time for this work. The first job is to make a temporary pool out of plastic or butyl sheeting in a shady spot — fill with pond water. Lift the marginal plants and the deep-water ones and put them in the temporary pool — now remove the floaters and oxygenators and put them in water-filled buckets or the temporary pool.

Begin to pump out the water. When shallow enough net the fish and place in a separate temporary pool — cover with fine netting. Finish draining the pond — lift up and divide any plants growing in the mud.

Remove the sludge layer and dump on vacant ground. Scrub the sides or use a pressure sprayer to remove the algae, taking care not to damage the surface. Refill the pond using tap water and replace the baskets of plants. After 3 or 4 days return the fish.

THE LEAKING POND

Don't assume your pond is cracked if the water level falls in summer. In hot and dry weather a drop of 1 - 2 cm in a week is quite normal

If the water level in your pond falls steadily in cool weather when the pump is switched off, then there is a hole or crack in the structure. You will have to let the water level fall to the source of the problem before carrying out the necessary repair. If the crack or hole is near the bottom of the pond it will be necessary to empty it before you can begin.

Repairing a concrete pond

The problem may be due to a porous surface because of the use of too much or the wrong type of sand or the presence of a large number of tiny cracks. The answer is to thoroughly clean the surface and then apply two coats of pond sealant. This repair should last for several years.

The other possibility is a distinct crack which is at least 1 cm wide. Undercut the crack with a cold chisel — the prepared crack should be wider below the surface. Remove all dust and fill with a waterproof mastic cement. Finally paint the area with a proprietary sealant. Large cracks are difficult to seal — it is usually better to fill with mortar and then fit a butyl liner.

Repairing a rigid liner pond

Vacuum-formed polyethylene ponds tend to crack after a few years because of the effect of sunlight. You can buy rigid liners guaranteed for 20 years, but even here cracks can appear if the edges are not firmly supported. Cracks are not always easy to locate — try tapping the surface and listening for a different note. Repair kits are available.

Repairing a flexible liner

Locating the crack or hole is not always easy. Press the surface after emptying — an unusually soft spot generally indicates a hole or tear in the liner. Flexible liners have a limited life span, varying from just a few years for cheap polyethylene to 50 years for top quality butyl sheeting.

It is not worth trying to repair a cracked polyethylene-lined pond — remove it and replace with PVC or butyl sheeting. If one of these better quality materials becomes torn or cracked you can buy a repair kit to seal the damaged area. Cut a piece of repair sheet which is twice as long and wide as the tear. Clean the patch and the pond sheeting and apply adhesive. Carefully follow the instructions on the kit package.

CHAPTER 3

GENERAL PROBLEMS

Chapter 2 dealt with the various specific problems which cause a garden to look unattractive and be clearly in need of revival. There could be trees which need removing or cutting back, a lawn which is full of weeds, or a border which is not the mass of colour you expect it to be. There are clear-cut ways of tackling these specific areas of disappointment and these are set out in the chapter beginning on page 4.

That is not the end of the story. Our feeling of disappointment with the garden may extend beyond a single area — it may cover the whole garden. Here we are concerned with general problems, and there are three basic types. First of all, there is the situation where the garden still looks good but is now beginning to deteriorate because you cannot cope with the work any more. If you do not do something to lessen the workload the garden will steadily get worse.

The second type of general problem is where the garden has lost its good looks because of a factor other than you — a factor which is not a short-term occurrence but has been going on for years. An example is a plot which has become uninteresting and short of colour — the effect may be due to poor design or plants which have been neglected by a previous owner. Revival methods are available (pages 67-70). There are a different set of rejuvenation techniques for the garden where animals are causing a general problem. Blackfly on broad beans and mildew on roses are specific problems, but rabbits will gnaw almost anything and cats will disturb bare ground in any bed, border or vegetable plot. Poor-quality soil is a much more serious difficulty as it affects millions of garden owners. Plant growth may suffer in your heavy or sandy ground and what you have to do is build up the crumb structure. The good news is that it need not cost you anything, but the bad news is that it might take several years.

Your garden may be colourful and the soil may be a fertile loam, but it may still disappoint you. A frequent complaint is that the garden is full of weeds in the lawn, beds, borders and pathways. A sprinkling of buttercups and daisies in the lawn is acceptable these days, but a noticeable cover of unsightly weeds in various parts of the garden certainly is not. There are both chemical and non-chemical methods of control — the section starting on page 61 will help you to choose which technique to use.

Weeds can be controlled but some of the causes of shade cannot — nearby buildings, tall fences, overhanging trees etc. Some of the shade problem can be reduced and there are also ways of either living with the situation or turning it into an advantage.

There is a third type of general problem which differs from the others by having a cause which occurs over a limited time period. Flooding is the most dramatic example as it can ruin a garden in a few hours, but it is fortunately rare. Drought is different — you can see the effect in millions of gardens after a few weeks of hot, dry weather. As with the other general problems there are avoidance and revival techniques which are described in this chapter.

" THE GARDEN IS JUST TOO MUCH WORK "

About half of all gardens belong to people who find gardening too much work. It may be that they are not interested and are therefore not willing to devote their leisure time to looking after the land around the house. There are also people who have just not enough time to look after the garden they love or they may no longer have the health and strength for active gardening.

For many the obvious course of paying someone else to do the work is not possible, and so the garden is neglected and becomes an eyesore. There is only one satisfactory answer if you cannot get help. You have to adopt a new way of gardening which reduces or eliminates all the great time wasters — digging, weeding, pruning and cutting the lawn edges. There is no magic formula for this — it is simply a matter of using the few basic principles set out below and the dos and don'ts on pages 57 - 60. Not many people can begin from scratch and bring in all of these time-saving features, but there is a great deal that can be done without much cost or effort in an established garden.

A final thought. A time-saving garden is a place of overall beauty — it is not an exhibition of individual showy blooms which must be regularly tended and cut once their charm starts to fade. Be tolerant — do not worry about the occasional weed in the lawn or the few plants which are not flourishing. The easy-care garden with its ground cover, year round colour, attractive paths and reliance on woody plants is often better to look at and not just easier to maintain than the traditional labour-intensive one.

THE 4 ESSENTIAL STEPS FOR A LABOUR-SAVING GARDEN

HAVE EASY-CARE FEATURES
page 57

GROW EASY-CARE PLANTS
pages 58 - 59

USE EASY-CARE AIDS
page 60

COVER THE GROUND
page 60

HAVE EASY-CARE FEATURES

Articles and books on garden design show you how to create an eye-catching garden with a professional look. Here design is taken from a different angle — this page shows you how to arrange the garden so that maintenance work is reduced to a minimum. Easy-care garden designs have one feature in common — hard (non-living) landscaping is important and soft landscaping (the use of plants) avoids types which need planting or sowing every year. However, don't be slavish about these things — of course you should have a hanging basket if it is a favourite feature, but remember it will mean a bit of extra work.

HARD LANDSCAPING

Hard landscaping is often a lot of work, but it can reduce the routine maintenance work that you have to do. Examples include the replacement of grass paths with bricks, gravel or stone slabs, the use of fences instead of hedges, the building of raised beds in the vegetable garden and the creation of a patio at the back of the house or in a spot where plants do not thrive.

BEDS & BORDERS

Get rid of the herbaceous border filled solely with hardy perennials — it involves a lot of work and looks bare and unsightly for half the year. Change to a mixed or shrub border — see page 13.

•

Avoid wide borders which have to be walked on to reach the plants at the back.

•

Avoid beds used for planting out annuals in a formal pattern.

CONTAINERS

One of the worst features for an easy-care garden. Regular watering is essential — once a day in hot and dry weather.

•

If you must have pots, choose large non-porous ones which reduce the need for frequent watering.

•

Do not use moss-lined hanging baskets — buy the type with a built-in water reservoir.

VEGETABLE PLOT

If you must have vegetables then avoid the allotment-type vegetable plot. It is much easier to grow them in narrow beds surrounded by gravel or bark — see page 24.

GREENHOUSE

The usual advice for the easy-care gardener is not to buy a greenhouse. If you feel it is worth the trouble, buy one made of low-maintenance material and do not aim to create hot house conditions.

ROCKERY

Rock gardens are hard work — regular weeding is essential and so is watering in dry weather. If you like alpines then grow them in a trough or in a raised bed.

LAWN

Have a narrow bare strip between the grass and the wall, fence etc so you can cut right up to the edge.

•

Keep the height of cut at 3 cm or more — mow every 2 weeks in season.

•

Do not aim for a luxury fine-grassed lawn — have a hard-wearing utility one.

•

Reduce or eliminate beds, trees and containers in the grass.

•

Consider getting rid of a small shady lawn and replacing it with paving if you are not devoted to grass.

•

Have curved corners rather than angled ones.

•

Water the front lawn if you must, but leave the back lawn alone in dry weather. It is better to save your watering time for annuals, newly-planted trees and shrubs.

GROW EASY-CARE PLANTS

In each group of plants there are easy-care examples which can be relied upon to give good results with a minimum of effort. With some groups, such as the ground cover plants, there are lots of varieties to choose from — with others, such as fruit trees and soft fruit bushes there are only a few which need little attention. Novelties are interesting, but as a general rule it is better to stick to the readily-available favourites which have proved themselves over the years. As a general plan, increase the number of trees and shrubs in the garden and reduce the area devoted to annuals, vegetables, bulbs which need lifting every year, small containers and fruit.

LOOK FOR THE EASY-CARE FEATURES

- **HARDY** *Frost-sensitive plants need winter protection or replacing in spring*
- **PERENNIAL** *Annuals need replacing every year*
- **EVERGREEN** *Deciduous shrubs and trees are bare in winter — fallen leaves need raking or sweeping*
- **GOOD DISEASE RESISTANCE** *Important with roses, asters, some vegetables etc. Check label or textbook*
- **PRUNING NOT VITAL** *Choose shrubs which do not need cutting back every year*
- **STAKING NOT NECESSARY** *Staking herbaceous border plants can be a chore — choose self-supporting types wherever possible*
- **SLOW GROWTH HABIT** *Plants which spread very rapidly often call for annual cutting back after a few years*

ANNUALS

The traditional way of using annuals is to bed out half-hardy types when the risk of frosts has gone and then lift them and throw them away. They provide instant colour in millions of gardens but use with care — planting out, dead-heading and regular watering because of the shallow root system can be a chore. Massed planting in formal patterns has no place in the easy-care garden — the best place is among other plants in a mixed border. The easiest and most economical way to grow annuals is to sprinkle seed lightly over the chosen area or to push large seeds of hardy annuals into the soil in spring.

PERENNIALS

The best place for hardy perennials is in a mixed border so that when they are dormant there are bulbs and evergreens to provide colour. Listed on page 15 are some easy-care ones — they are fully hardy, do not need lifting and dividing every few years, are not regularly affected by disease and do not need staking.

ROSES

Roses are a delight, but they call for an appreciable amount of work — pruning, dead-heading, spraying etc. Mildew and black spot can be a menace — always choose varieties with good disease resistance. The small-leaved ground cover roses are trouble-free. Prune roses the easy but extremely effective way. Just cut out any dead and very thin branches in autumn and then in late winter cut down all the remaining branches of hybrid teas and floribundas by one half.

FRUIT

Choose with care. A few are no more trouble than any straightforward ornamental tree or shrub, but others involve a lot of hard work. Easy-care types include apples on dwarfing rootstocks, thornless blackberries, autumn raspberries, red and white currants, and strawberries grown in barrels.

BULBS

Bulbs are excellent subjects for the easy-care garden if you choose the right types. Avoid the ones which have to be lifted and stored each year — hyacinths, garden tulips and gladioli. Plant the ones which can be left in the ground to come up year after year — daffodils, species tulips, crocuses, snowdrops etc. One of the best ways to use bulbs is to naturalise them in rough grassland or woodland. In the lawn you can't cut the grass until the leaves have turned brown and withered.

VEGETABLES

Vegetables are not a good idea as a lot of work is involved, but you can grow some quite easily between flowers and shrubs. If you want a vegetable plot try the bed system — see page 24. Nearly all herbs are easy to grow. They should be cropped little and often, and rampant spreaders such as mint must be kept in check.

TREES & SHRUBS

Trees and shrubs have a vital role to play in any garden. They provide the basic skeleton and give the area a feeling of maturity. Evergreens and the winter-flowering ones provide interest when the rest of the garden is asleep and we rely on hedges for privacy. For the gardener who wants to save work there is an additional virtue — they are much less trouble than annuals, perennials, vegetables, lawns and fruit. Once fully established there is little work to be done with most of them — no annual replanting or sowing ritual, no regular feeding or spraying. No staking or dead-heading and no rushing out with the watering can. When buying new ones you should check that they possess most if not all the properties in the check-list on page 58. You have to be careful when making your choice — there are types which need careful pruning every year and there are others which need winter protection. Some spread quickly and others soon get out of hand. Easy-care examples are listed below.

Abies	Cotoneaster	Hamamelis	Mahonia	Ribes
Acer	Crataegus	Hebe	Osmanthus	Robinia
Aucuba	Daphne	Hedera	Parthenocissus	Salix
Berberis	Elaeagnus	Hydrangea	Phormium	Skimmia
Betula	Erica	Hypericum	Pieris	Sorbus
Carpinus	Escallonia	Ilex	Pinus	Spiraea
Chaenomeles	Euonymus	Jasminum	Potentilla	Taxus
Chamaecyparis	Garrya	Juniperus	Prunus	Thuja
Choisya	Gaultheria	Lavandula	Pyracantha	Viburnum
Cotinus	Genista	Lonicera	Rhododendron	Vinca

GROUND COVER PLANTS

In the easy-care garden it is essential to cover bare ground to reduce or eliminate the weed problem. One way to do this is to grow ground cover plants — these are reasonably or highly ornamental plants with a spread of leafy growth which is sufficiently dense to inhibit weed development. Most but not all are low-growing and most but not all are evergreen. Use them around trees and large shrubs and to clothe inaccessible areas such as steep banks where vigorous invasive types are a godsend. Ground cover plants are useful but do not try to fill all the bare spaces with ground cover plants rather than a mulch — if you do the garden will have an overcrowded look. Listed below are popular examples.

Ajuga	Epimedium	Hedera	Lamium	Pulmonaria
Alchemilla	Euonymus	Hosta	Lysimachia	Rosa
Ballota	Euphorbia	Hypericum	Nepeta	Sedum
Bergenia	Geranium	Iberis	Pachysandra	Stachys
Cotoneaster	Hebe	Juniperus	Polygonum	Vinca

The high-maintenance garden — a riot of colour in summer but there is a regular round of planting, trimming, watering and dead-heading

The low-maintenance garden — a combination of easy-care plants, a weed-controlling mulch and a lawn designed for easy cutting

USE EASY-CARE AIDS

Time-saving pieces of equipment are essential for the easy-care gardener, but they must be affordable and also truly useful. Some so-called 'aids' actually make more work than the simple tools they replace. Choose carefully — much time and effort is wasted by using the wrong equipment. A spade which is just right for a strong youth would be quite wrong for a small frail lady. Try before you buy. For the elderly and the handicapped picking the right tools is even more important — it can mean the difference between being able to do a task or not. Finally, keep equipment clean, sharp and oiled if necessary.

A power cultivator may seem a good idea, but in a small ornamental garden it may not be worth while. A good idea if you are making a new garden or creating a bed in uncultivated ground — consider hiring one rather than buying a new model.

•

There are all sorts of aids for the infirm and the elderly — long-handled versions of grabbers, bulb planters, forks, trowels etc, and 2-wheeled or 4-wheeled carts instead of wheelbarrows.

•

Watering with a can or hose is one of the most time-consuming of all gardening jobs. Invest if you can in an overall watering system — look at sprinklers, seep hoses and automatic systems.

The use of a long-lasting weedkiller will remove the chore of having to pull out weeds from a gravel path.

•

Automatic ventilators and automatic watering in the greenhouse are a great boon.

•

A hedge trimmer is a wise investment if you have a long hedge to cut — make sure it is not too heavy for comfort.

•

There is no point in spraying unless it is vital. If it is required (weeds on paths, greenfly invasion on roses etc) use a ready-to-use trigger-operated brand. More costly, but a great time saver.

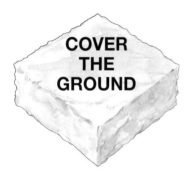

COVER THE GROUND

Covering the ground around the plants is one of the most important yet neglected gardening techniques, and for the easy-care garden it is doubly important. Leaving the soil uncovered will inevitably lead to a weed problem and all the work involved in trying to get rid of them. Walking on bare earth will often lead to a surface capping problem. Ground cover is the answer and there are three alternative approaches. You can use a humus mulch to improve the soil structure and cut down the need to weed and water, a weed control mulch to prevent weed growth, or ground cover plants to improve appearance and inhibit weed seed germination.

Humus mulch
page 78

Weed control mulch
page 63

Ground cover plants
page 59

" THE GARDEN SEEMS TO BE FULL OF WEEDS "

Weeding is the most disliked of all gardening jobs and in most gardens it is tackled badly. Little is done to prevent the arrival of weeds and when they become unsightly we spend hours hoeing, forking out and hand pulling. We then find that the first bed we treated is full of weeds again by the time we reach the last bed or border.

There is practically no way of completely protecting your garden from weed attack but you can do much better than the routine above. The way to tackle the problem is to follow the correct routine for your situation — see the following pages. Before that you must understand the difference between annual and perennial weeds — see below.

ANNUAL OR PERENNIAL?

Annual Weeds Ⓐ

Annual weeds complete at least one life cycle from seed to seed during the season. They spread by seeding, and all fertile soils contain a large reservoir of annual weed seeds. The golden rule is that emerged annual weeds must be killed before they produce seeds — kill them by hand pulling, digging out, hoeing or by burning off with a contact weedkiller.

Perennial Weeds Ⓟ

Perennial weeds survive by means of underground stems or roots which act as storage organs over winter. Dig out the whole plant including the root if you can. Otherwise the leaves must be regularly removed to make the garden look tidy and perhaps weaken the weeds, or else use a translocated weedkiller which travels to the underground parts and so kills the plant.

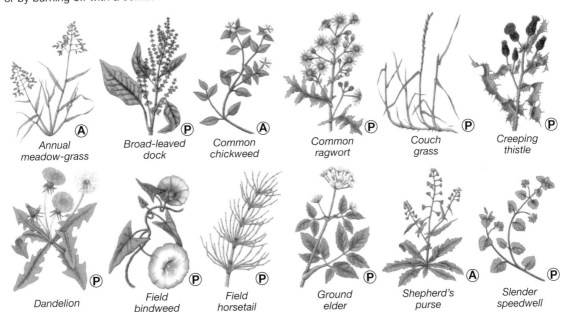

Ⓐ Annual meadow-grass

Ⓟ Broad-leaved dock

Ⓐ Common chickweed

Ⓟ Common ragwort

Ⓟ Couch grass

Ⓟ Creeping thistle

Ⓟ Dandelion

Ⓟ Field bindweed

Ⓟ Field horsetail

Ⓟ Ground elder

Ⓐ Shepherd's purse

Ⓟ Slender speedwell

WEEDS BETWEEN GARDEN PLANTS

Weeding beds and borders is often an endless chore. A few annual types growing between the shrubs or border plants offer no problem, but perennial weeds growing inside plant clumps or twining up the shoots are a real problem

Non-chemical methods of control

Hoeing is the traditional method of control — it will effectively kill annuals when done properly, but it has no long-term effect on perennial ones. These need grubbing out — see below. The proper way to use a hoe depends on the type.

Choose a day when the soil surface is dry — aim to sever the weed stems rather then merely dragging them out. Hoe with care. Roots of some plants lie close to the surface and much damage can be done by hoeing too deeply. Don't hoe if weeds are absent as disturbing the soil brings up a fresh crop of weed seeds. A golden rule — do not let the weeds get out of hand before hoeing. Do this work regularly. Keep the blade clean and sharp.

•

Grubbing out is the way to tackle perennial weeds. Never grasp the stem and pull sharply — the usual result is for the stem to come away and the roots to stay in the ground, enabling the weed to re-sprout quite happily. Grub out by loosening the soil around the weed with a garden or hand fork. Pull up the weed gently and steadily so that the main roots remain attached.

•

Perennial weeds growing within a flowering plant clump in the border pose a problem. You may be able to gently pull out the weeds but this is usually not possible. The only thing to do is to lift the clump in autumn and divide it into segments for replanting, removing all the weed roots before you do so.

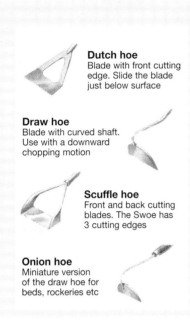

Dutch hoe
Blade with front cutting edge. Slide the blade just below surface

Draw hoe
Blade with curved shaft. Use with a downward chopping motion

Scuffle hoe
Front and back cutting blades. The Swoe has 3 cutting edges

Onion hoe
Miniature version of the draw hoe for beds, rockeries etc

Chemical methods of control

There are basically two types of products for use around growing plants. Weedkillers based on paraquat/diquat act as a chemical hoe, killing the top growth of weeds within a few days. Quick-acting, but the roots are not harmed and so they are not effective against perennial weeds.

•

Glyphosate and glufosinate ammonium go down to the roots and so both perennial and annual weeds are killed. They are slower acting than paraquat/diquat and may take several weeks to work. It may be necessary to repeat the treatment later in the season.

•

Both paraquat/diquat and glyphosate will kill garden plants as well as weeds so you must keep the spray away from the foliage of shrubs, flowers, vegetables etc. Use a ready-to-use spray or diluted spray in a watering can fitted with a dribble bar. Work as close to the weeds as possible. Never use weedkiller spraying equipment for any other purpose. Choose a still day when the weeds are actively growing in late spring or summer.

•

The most difficult situation is where the weeds are growing next to flowers and shrubs or twining up their stems. It is safer to use glyphosate gel here rather than a spray — apply it to the weed leaves with the brush provided or put some of the weedkiller on the thumb and forefinger of a rubber glove and stroke the leaves. Bindweed can be a serious nuisance. Insert a cane well above the height of the plant and allow the weed to climb up it — treat as shown in the illustration on the right.

Prevention

Ground cover

Without preventive measures you are sure to have weeds appearing in the soil around your plants. Soil-borne and air-borne seeds will make it inevitable, and so will buried roots of perennial weeds. You can help matters by cutting down the area of bare earth. This can be done by setting bedding plants more closely together than usual, by adopting the bed method of growing vegetables (see page 24) or by planting a low-growing evergreen ground cover such as Ajuga reptans (see photograph on the left).

•

Weed control mulch

A weed control mulch is an excellent but under-used method of weed prevention. It is a layer of weed-proof material which is usually covered with a layer of gravel, stone chippings, pea shingle, pebbles or shredded bark to give a decorative surface. There are three materials from which to make your choice — opened-up cardboard boxes can be used but they are not long-lasting like the basic three.

Black polyethylene sheeting is widely available and is the most popular type of weed control mulch. Standard 150 - 200 gauge will only last a single season if it is not covered with gravel or bark to keep out sunlight — heavy-duty 500 gauge sheeting will last for several years even if there is no lightproof cover.

Woven polypropylene is harder to find than polyethylene and is about 3 times the price. It is used in the same way, but has the added advantage of letting water seep through the myriad holes between the threads rather than having to percolate through the edges of the sheet. It will last for 6 years or more.

Old carpeting may seem an odd choice for use in the garden but it makes an excellent weed control mulch — use it as a strip between rows of plants or cut into squares and use as tree spats (see below). It is easy to lay, but a surface cover is essential. Long lasting, and of course free when you decide to recarpet a room.

•

Mulching around plants

The area close to the stems is the most difficult to hoe but it is also the most important to keep weed-free when establishing a new specimen. Cut pieces of sheeting and place around the plants — make sure the edges overlap. Non bio-degradable plastic bags can be used to cover small areas.

A newly-planted tree grows more slowly if grassy weeds are allowed to grow around the base. To keep this area weed-free place a felt-based tree spat around the trunk.

•

Mulching before planting

Weed control mulching really comes into its own on ground which is to be planted — done properly it will mean that weeding will be a thing of the past. This type of mulching is perhaps most successful when you are making a new shrub border, although it can be used for a mixed border. It can also be used in the vegetable plot where growth is stimulated, potatoes no longer need earthing up and strawberries, marrows and courgettes are kept off the ground.

September is a good time to put down the mulch for autumn planting of roses etc, but with the vegetable plot you will have to put down the mulch in spring. The first step is to cut down and remove tall weeds — you can spray with glyphosate if there is a lot of unwanted growth. Fork a fertilizer into the soil if it is poor. Use polyethylene or polypropylene sheeting — make sure each sheet overlaps the one below. Bury the edges in the soil and make slits or cross cuts on the surface to act as planting holes.

Exposed plastic sheeting may be acceptable in the vegetable plot but some form of cover is needed in the ornamental garden. Water will move effectively between the sheets and through the slits, but prick the sheets in areas where puddles form.

WEEDS ON BARE GROUND

There is no 'best' method for getting rid of weeds on a bare patch of ground. It depends on the amount and type of weeds present and the proposed use of land

Non-chemical methods of control

If there is a scattering of annual weeds and a few isolated perennial weeds you should not have a problem. Gently ease out the perennials with a fork and then hoe the annual ones — see 'Weeds between growing plants' (page 62) to learn the proper way to do this.

Digging is the traditional answer if the weed cover is reasonably heavy. Invert each spadeful to bury the annual weeds and then remove all the roots of perennial weeds you can find in the turned-over block of soil. Digging is hard work and not particularly effective against the difficult perennials such as couch grass, bindweed and ground elder. Consider the spraying alternative — see below.

If the ground is covered with a dense mat of weeds and grass you will need an alternative method to digging. By far the best plan is to cover the weedy ground with strips of plastic sheeting which is then pegged down and covered with gravel or bark chippings. For details see 'Weeds between growing plants — Prevention' on page 63. After one or a couple of seasons the weeds will be killed. No problem if you have no plans for the soil, but if you plan to put in shrubs or roses it will be necessary to spray with glyphosate (see below) and then plant through a weed control mulch — see page 63.

Chemical methods of control

A glyphosate-based weedkiller is the product to use. It travels down into the roots and so kills both annual and perennial weeds rather than merely burning off the tops. It works quite slowly, so don't expect too much for a few weeks. Apply on a still day when the weeds are growing actively — choose a ready-to-use spray for a small area but you will need to use diluted glyphosate in a hand-held or knapsack sprayer if the weedy patch is extensive. Glyphosate breaks down on contact with the soil so there is no residual action.

Sodium chlorate is the weedkiller which will keep the land weed-free all season. Use with care — any drift or creep of the spray on to beds, borders or turf can be disastrous. Do not use near to trees and buy a product with a fire suppressant.

Prevention

Planting the area with closely-spaced evergreen ground cover plants will not give the same degree of control as a weed control mulch or a long-lasting residual weedkiller like sodium chlorate, but it will suppress most annual weeds. Euonymus fortunei is an example (see left) — for a list of recommended ground covering plants see page 59. Remove perennial weed roots before planting.

The weed control mulch described on page 63 can be used on bare ground to prevent weed growth. Alternatively you can spray with sodium chlorate.

WEEDS ON PATHS

Weeds growing in the cracks between paving stones or on the surface of gravel paths give the garden an uncared-for look, but trying to pull them out by hand is not the answer

Non-chemical methods of control

The best tool to use for getting rid of weeds growing in the cracks is a weeding knife — see the illustration on the left. The first step is to slice down either side with the blade edges of the knife to cut through the roots and then turn the blade over. Push the blade point down into the ground and then hook below the weed — lift up to remove it.

A flame gun is a useful tool for killing the top-growth of weeds in paths if you do not want to use a chemical. Two things to remember. You must wear protective goggles if you are treating a gravel path and you should not try to burn the weeds to extinction. Even a brief exposure of the weed's growing point to the flame will result in it shrivelling up within a few days.

Chemical methods of control

Both paraquat/diquat and glyphosate can be used to kill weeds on paths and patios — glyphosate will kill perennial as well as annual weeds but neither of them has any residual effect.

A proprietary path weedkiller is a better choice — this mixture of active ingredients will kill existing weeds and give you extended protection against further invasion. Some brands kill perennial as well as annual weeds. With all path weedkillers it is essential to follow the precautions. Avoid run-off on to surrounding lawns or beds and do not walk from the path onto turf immediately after treatment.

Prevention

The essential step is when a path or patio is being laid. A weed-preventing layer must be placed below the paving material — slabs, gravel, bricks etc must never be laid on bare earth. Path weedkillers will provide protection on existing paths — see above.

WEEDS IN LAWNS

People are less fussy these days about buttercups and daisies in the lawn, but some weeds are really unsightly and there are others which can become a menace if allowed to spread. Carefully grub out individual weeds or spray with a suitable weedkiller if the problem is widespread — see the section on lawns on page 12 for a control programme or The Lawn Expert for details of individual weeds

" THE GARDEN IS PLAIN AND THERE'S NO COLOUR "

One point has to be made at the outset. There is nothing wrong with a plain garden. A simple rectangular lawn with a fringe of narrow borders is not a 'wrong' design as long as it is cared for and as long as it pleases you and the family. However, it may be that you have moved house and inherited a plain garden which is not to your taste, or perhaps you have grown tired of the dull appearance of the garden you have had for many years. Then it is time to change, and the purpose of this section is to suggest various ways to enliven the design and add both colour and interest to your plot.

FEATURES OF THE PLAIN GARDEN

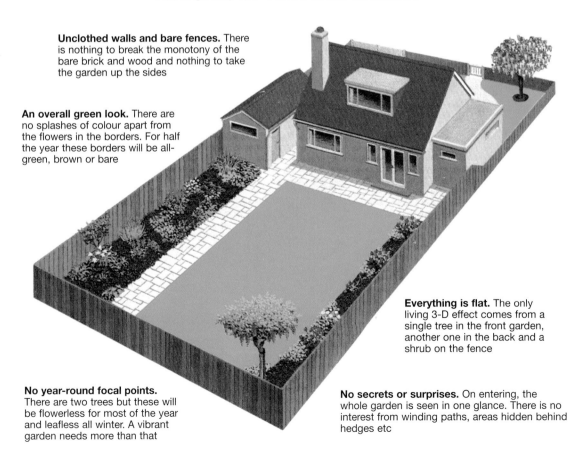

Unclothed walls and bare fences. There is nothing to break the monotony of the bare brick and wood and nothing to take the garden up the sides

An overall green look. There are no splashes of colour apart from the flowers in the borders. For half the year these borders will be all-green, brown or bare

Everything is flat. The only living 3-D effect comes from a single tree in the front garden, another one in the back and a shrub on the fence

No year-round focal points. There are two trees but these will be flowerless for most of the year and leafless all winter. A vibrant garden needs more than that

No secrets or surprises. On entering, the whole garden is seen in one glance. There is no interest from winding paths, areas hidden behind hedges etc

LIVEN UP THE DESIGN

The basic cause of an uninteresting design is the absence of areas which are fully or partly hidden when you look at the garden from the house. These areas may be protected from view by fences, hedges, walls or screening plants. Adding to the dull look is a lack of change in levels, a lack of focal points and an abundance of straight lines. Winding paths are generally more interesting than straight ones and round or irregular-shaped beds may be more appealing than oblong ones, but do not be tempted to move from an over-plain design to an over-fussy one.

WINGS & MINIGARDENS

A wing is a portion of the border which is extended to break the line of the lawn. The back of this wing is hidden from the house, and so the whole garden can no longer be seen at a glance. A minigarden is a section of the garden which is partly or wholly separated by some form of barrier — in a small plot it may be a simple fence to enclose a play area and in a grand garden you may find hedge-enclosed garden rooms which have to be entered to be seen. These pockets can provide a partly hidden element which is so essential if you want to add interest to your garden.

ADDED HEIGHT

Height and changing levels add interest, but countless gardens look dull because everything seems so flat. All the plants are in the ground at the same level and apart from a few trees everything seems to grow to be ankle-high, knee-high or waist-high. In addition nearly all the non-living features are at eye-level or below — you never have to look upwards to enjoy the garden. Fortunately there are many ways to remove this feeling of flatness — decorative trees and tall shrubs are the most important source of added height, but see pages 68 - 70 for other ideas.

FOCAL POINTS

A focal point is an object which on its own catches the attention of the observer — ideally focal points should be far enough apart for you to have to move your gaze from one to the other, but it may not be possible in a small garden. Installing focal points is one of the most effective ways of adding interest to a dull garden and there are numerous types from which to make your choice — see pages 68 - 70.

CURVES

Curves are generally more interesting than straight lines in garden design, but there are no hard-and-fast rules — professional designs usually incorporate both. There are a few guidelines you should follow. Curves should be flowing, simple and geometrical — a series of odd-shaped bends and twists should be avoided. A curving path should lead somewhere — to a seat, gate or focal point. The path can be smoothly serpentine (snake-like) but in the area inside each curve there should be a feature or planting to give the bend some purpose.

LIVEN UP THE PLANTING

Lack of colour and lack of interest often but not always go together. A skilful planting of attractive white-flowering shrubs and perennials would lack colour but could look quite stunning, but a bed of marigolds edged with alyssum would be colourful but might not warrant a second glance. The planting in a bed or border needs both shape and colour for maximum effect. Beds and borders are only part of the story. There should be specimen plants to serve as focal points, climbing plants to add height to the display and flower-filled containers to add touches of colour.

CLIMBERS & WALL PLANTS

It is surprising how effective climbers and wall plants can be in improving the look of a garden. The reason is that they provide two essentials for an attractive garden — height and colour. Plant scramblers such as honeysuckle to clamber through trees, grow roses or Wisteria against walls and clothe arches with Clematis. Use wall plants such as Pyracantha to remove the bareness at the bottom of house walls. The most important sites for climbers are bare fences and the walls around the back and front door. These plants will make you look upwards as well as from side to side.

UNDERPLANTING

The ground under many trees can be used for growing plants to provide added colour and interest, but it can be tricky. All trees will cast shade and they will draw heavily on the soil reserves of nutrients and water, so it is necessary to choose carefully and water in dry weather. Suitable plants for underplanting include Vinca, Sarcococca, Hedera, Aucuba, Cyclamen, Geranium, Euphorbia, Pachysandra and Tiarella.

EXTENDED DISPLAY

Few gardens are dull all year round — the usual problem is that the floral display is rather short-lived and the garden looks drab because the plants have not been chosen to provide a year-round display. You need some trees to provide the permanent skeleton and you need some evergreens to give winter colour. Coloured-leaf evergreens can be a great help — see page 69. Another anti-dull technique is to look for shrubs with an extended display. Pyracantha is a typical example — glossy evergreen leaves, white flowers in June and coloured berries in autumn.

CONTAINERS

Plants in containers are one of the basic ways of brightening up a dull garden. Favourite areas are patios, window sills, balconies, doorways and stairways. The range of containers is even more extensive — pots, tubs, hanging baskets, window boxes, sinks etc. There are no absolute rules but a few guidelines may be useful. Try to choose a container style, surface and material which are in keeping with the surroundings and let either the container or plant display be the centre of attention. A perfectly plain pot calls for a showy display — a large ornate urn should have a simple one.

ARCHITECTURAL PLANTS

An architectural plant is a grass, tree or shrub which is attractive enough or interesting enough to serve as a focal point. It can be grown on its own in a container or in the lawn, or set in the border to provide an eye-catching feature beside the run-of-the-mill resident plants. There is no single property which separates architectural plants from the others. Some have an appealing sculptured shape such as a mature Rhus, and others are grown for their large leaves or flower heads — Catalpa, Gunnera, Cortaderia, Ailanthus and so on. It may be palm-like (e.g Cordyline) or may have attractive bark (e.g Prunus serrula). Large-leaved succulents such as Agave belong here and so do the exotic-looking tropical plants such as Musa, Hedychium, Grevillea and Dicksonia.

COLOUR

Your garden lacks colour so naturally you think about improving the floral display. Books on garden design will give you all sorts of instructions on the proper use of colour, but few of these guidelines are actual rules. Dazzling bright colours or gentle pastel shades — it really is up to you. If pink next to orange doesn't offend you then go ahead and put those plants together. But there are some principles which you should heed. Warm colours (yellow, orange and red) make the flowers look closer than they really are — the cool ones (green and blue) make the flowers look further away. To make a plot look longer, plant warm-colour flowers close to the house and set the cool colours right at the back. Large splashes of single colours are more dramatic than a mass of small spots of various colours. Be careful not to overdo your quest for more colour — a brightly-coloured window box with blooms in delicate shades of pink or violet can look an eyesore.

It is not wise to rely solely on flowers to provide living colour. Their display is short-lived and for most of the year you are looking at leaves and stems — it is usually in the late autumn and winter months when people are most dissatisfied with the colour in their garden. To overcome this problem bring in plants with coloured foliage, especially evergreen ones which will provide colour in the out-of-season months when other plants are bare. In the photograph above there are virtually no flowers and yet the border is full of colour. Some of the shrubs are evergreen, and so the red, yellow and green display lasts all year. The plants providing the display are Ballota pseudodictamnus, Berberis thunbergii 'Atropurpurea', Choisya ternata 'Sundance', Euonymus fortunei 'Emerald 'n Gold', Geranium, Ribes sanguineum 'Brocklebankii', Robinia pseudoacacia 'Frisia', Salix integra 'Hakuro Nishiki', Stachys byzantica and Weigela florida foliis purpureus.

LIVEN UP THE FEATURES

The basic component of a feature-starved garden is generally an over-large lawn which dominates the scene. It is not a matter of actual size — you can see an over-large lawn in front of a modest house or around a country estate. For nearly everyone grass is a vital feature, but it should share the stage with a number of other features if you want an interesting garden which your friends will admire rather than a purely restful one for your own enjoyment. The features you need include both non-living and living ones — for details on the role of plants see pages 68 - 69.

FOCAL POINTS

The value of focal points is described on page 67, and the way to use architectural plants to provide eye-catching touches is set out on page 69. But you should also consider the wide range of non-living features which can serve as focal points. There are decorative containers which may or may not be filled with plants, and there are all sorts of seats, arches, summer houses, statues, fountains, pergolas and so on. Unfortunately not all focal points are attractive — there may be an offensive one over the fence. Create your own attractive one nearby to divert attention.

WATER

Water has a magical quality — no garden could be really dull if it has an attractive water feature. Plants, fish and fountain may be the ideal, but this combination may not be practical in a small plot. Miniponds involve a constant battle against green algae, and so it is worth while to think about an alternative. There are easy ways to treat the water to keep it clear if you install a small fountain or a decorative stone unit which incorporates a mini-waterfall.

ADDED HEIGHT

Creating a change in the level at which plants are grown provides instant interest. Using tall pots, window boxes and hanging baskets (see page 68) is obvious — not so obvious is the creation of raised beds. The walling material should blend in with the surroundings. Adding this third dimension livens up a flat site, but there are additional advantages — drainage is improved in heavy soil, small plants are brought closer to the eye and jobs such as planting and weeding are made easier. Rockeries and raised patios are other ways of relieving the dullness of an all-over flat garden.

PAVING

Creating a paved area with reconstituted stone slabs which is then furnished with table, chairs and flower-filled containers will break up the lawn/bed/border pattern and add new life to the garden. There is no rule that this must be next to the house — there are advantages in moving it to a quieter and perhaps more attractive area of your plot. This patio approach is not the only way to use paving. A paved circle of ornamental bricks or setts makes an excellent base for the focal point you have chosen — a sundial, birdbath, statue or small water feature at its centre.

" WILDLIFE'S FINE, BUT IT'S SPOILING MY GARDEN "

The idea of wildlife visiting the garden always seems so desirable. Butterflies, dragonflies, birds, frogs, hedgehogs — there are many books to tell you how to make your garden even more attractive to them. But there is a downside – one of the most destructive forces in rural areas is a small group of animals which comes to the garden to eat or harm our plants rather than to please us.

The effect can be quite distressing. A few moles can create havoc overnight in the lawn — a wandering deer can strip all the young growth from a bed of roses in just a single day. Unfortunately control is more difficult than getting rid of the greenfly on the roses. Creating a barrier is impossible for some animal intruders and difficult for the others, and poisoning is certainly not a general option.

The usual approach to control is to protect the plants and/or discourage the invading animals without harming them — a fruit cage is an example. There are exceptions — rats must be killed and moles too if all else fails. Finally, there are animals like the squirrel which we just have to live with.

BIRDS

Seeds and seedlings are eaten, vegetables such as peas and brassicas may have their leaves torn, flowers (e.g crocus, polyanthus) and buds of some shrubs (e.g Forsythia) may be stripped. It is the fruit garden which suffers most of all. Bullfinches and sparrows devour buds of cherries, gooseberries etc and ripening fruit may disappear. Protection methods depend on the plants under threat. Cover seeds with tunnels made with small-mesh plastic-coated wire netting. Small areas of fruit can be protected by soft netting draped over canes — a large number of fruit bushes calls for a fruit cage. Spray-on repellents are of limited value and mechanical scarers soon lose their deterrent value.

CATS

Cats are a pest if they decide to use your garden as a toilet. A patch of dry bare earth is the favourite site and so the best way to keep them away is to cover as much of the ground as possible with plants. This cannot be done in the traditional vegetable plot — here the seedlings have to be protected with wire netting, fleece or cuttings from prickly plants. Deterrents include moth balls, lemon peel, pepper, modern chemicals and sonic deterrents, but there is no fool-proof method of protection.

DEER

Our native deer have always been an occasional problem, but the introduction of the dog-sized muntjac has created havoc in many rural areas close to woodland. Woody shoots are severed, bark on trees is gnawed away and young growth on shrubs is stripped. Fencing at least 2 m high is the best answer but it not usually practical. Protect newly-planted trees with tree guards — put fine-mesh wire netting around established ones. Deterrent sprays have limited value.

DOGS

Dogs, like cats, will disturb the ground where plants are growing, but the serious effect is the scorch caused by their urine. Conifers etc are damaged by dogs — lawns are disfigured by bitches. There is no really satisfactory answer — deterrents are of limited value. The only thing you can do is to drench the area immediately with a couple of buckets of water, but this is often not practical. With your own bitch make sure to train her from an early age to choose an area away from the lawn.

MICE & RATS

Other animals are often blamed for the damage caused by mice. Large seeds such as peas and sweet corn are dug out and small bulbs and corms such as crocus are removed. Between autumn and spring they will come indoors to eat stored fruit and vegetables. Proprietary mouse baits are effective and old-fashioned mouse traps are available — read the instructions for guidance on pet protection. Rats rather than mice may be responsible for apple damage in store — contact your local council.

MOLES

Borders and beds as well as lawns may be harmed — see page 11.

RABBITS

A serious problem in rural areas. Flowers, shrubs and vegetables are nibbled and bark may be gnawed. There is no easy answer. Tree guards will protect individual woody plants, but deterrents soon lose their power and ordinary fences are ineffective. A rabbit fence uses 1.5 m wire netting with the bottom 30 cm buried below ground. They can be shot, trapped or gassed, but many people find this distasteful and it rarely fully solves the problem. Lists of 'resistant' plants are not always reliable.

SQUIRRELS

Nice to watch and always welcome in the garden, but they can be a nuisance and their damage is often blamed on rabbits. They eat bulbs, nibble shoot tips, remove flower buds, carry away soft fruit and strip bark off the base of trees. As with rabbits there is no simple solution and drastic measures like trapping are out of the question. Anti-rabbit tree guards will protect woody plants against squirrel attack and secure net-covered cages can be used for groups of plants if there is a serious problem.

" THE SOIL IS AWFUL AND PLANTS DON'T THRIVE "

Can you show me how to improve my soil? There are two occasions when this plea is made — when a garden has just been taken over and the plants aren't growing properly, or when a garden owner is no longer willing to put up with the failures and disappointments which occur every year.

You can pick from many thousands of garden plants and you can select from all sorts of garden designs, but you have to settle for the soil you have. If it is in poor condition you will be involved with extra work and expense. The plant display will be disappointing — in addition the lack of vigorous growth and spread means that a considerable amount of ground cover will be needed to cover the bare spaces around the shrubs and perennials. Some newly-planted specimens will fail, and so there is the extra cost and effort of replacement.

Something has to be done, and unfortunately there is no simple miracle cure for everyone. A sprinkle of fertilizer may be all that is necessary, but in nearly every case the problem is more complex. Your first job is to spend a little time looking at the site. Are worms absent in the soil .... organic matter is lacking. Are the leaves of lime-hating plants yellow .... the soil is alkaline. Does water stand on the surface after rain .... you have a drainage problem. Are nettles growing vigorously .... the soil is well supplied with nitrogen. The remaining job is to work on each of the four steps involved in good soil management. The basic principle is twofold — improve things which can be changed and try to select plants which will flourish in your non-perfect soil.

THE 4 ESSENTIAL STEPS TO GOOD SOIL MANAGEMENT

IMPROVING THE SOIL
pages 74 - 75

CHOOSING CAREFULLY
pages 76 - 77

MULCHING
page 78

FEEDING
page 79

IMPROVING THE SOIL

If you are very lucky you will have a loamy soil which is nearly neutral, and that means that it is neither strongly acid nor alkaline. Working it will be as easy as it seems on TV gardening programmes and almost all plants will flourish if the nutrient levels are satisfactory and the light requirements are met. Unfortunately most soils are either clayey or sandy and need to be improved if the plants are suffering. As noted below there is no quick answer and no chemical product which can transform structureless soil into loam. Various techniques are involved but the essential one is the incorporation of organic matter. Liming helps in some soils and digging allows winter's frosts to break up clods of clay, but only humus can create the crumbly soil you desire.

SOIL TYPES

LOAM

This is the type of soil which is ideal — it is neither noticeably clayey nor sandy. It is the right texture but there may still be an acidity or alkalinity problem — see below

Maintain the vital organic content by putting on a mulch every spring and then digging it into the surface soil in autumn.

HEAVY (Clayey) SOIL

Squeeze a handful of moist soil. It forms a strong ball — when pressed it changes shape but does not fall apart. This ball feels smooth and sticky when wet. Stains the skin

Good points: Generally well supplied with plant foods which are not leached away by rain. Good water retention.

Bad points: Difficult to cultivate under most conditions. Cakes and cracks in dry weather — may waterlog in wet weather. Cold — flowers and vegetables appear later than average.

●

If the plot has not been cultivated before then dig thoroughly in autumn (see page 75) to expose the clods to winter frost — a generous quantity of bulky organic matter should be incorporated at this time. Apply lime if the soil is acid or gypsum if it is not to improve the structure. Do not plant out until the soil is reasonably dry. Mulch established plants. Each autumn fork organic matter into the top 15 cm of soil. Do not expect miracles — it will take 3 - 5 years to create a crumbly structure.

LIGHT (Sandy) SOIL

Squeeze a handful of moist soil. When released it sifts through the fingers. A small sample feels gritty when rubbed between finger and thumb. Does not stain the skin

Good points: Easy to work, even when wet. Free-draining in winter. Warm — suitable for early flowers and vegetables.

Bad points: Usually short of plant foods. Frequent watering is necessary in summer or shallow-rooted plants may die. Cools down rapidly at night.

●

Water and food shortage are regular problems during the growing season. The structure is generally poor — lack of organic matter means that the soil is not crumbly. Digging is not the answer — if you decide to dig then do it in spring, not autumn. The solution is to incorporate plenty of humus-making material into the top 10 - 15 cm in late winter or early spring — tread down the soil after cultivating. Mulching is vital to conserve moisture and reduce the leaching of plant nutrients. Grow ground-cover plants.

ACID SOIL

Test with a pH meter available from your garden centre. Nearly all easy-care plants will grow quite happily in mildly acid soil

Good points: Acid soil is required for azalea, camellia, blue hydrangea, most heathers, pieris, rhododendron and fine lawn grass.

Bad points: Bacterial and earthworm activity are reduced in distinctly acid soil and many plants suffer under such conditions.

●

Grow acid-loving plants — for others it is necessary to add a dressing of lime if the pH meter indicates very acid soil.

ALKALINE SOIL

Test with a pH meter available from your garden centre. Nearly all easy-care plants will grow quite happily in mildly alkaline soil

Good points: Lime-rich soil is satisfactory for carnation, wallflower, delphinium, scabious, cabbage, some shrubs and many alpines.

Bad points: Plant foods are locked up in alkaline soils and the leaves of acid-loving plants such as rhododendron turn yellow.

●

Avoid plants which require an acid soil. Existing acid-loving plants should be treated with a fertilizer containing sequestrene.

HUMUS MAKERS — THE MATERIALS WHICH TURN CLAY OR SAND INTO SOIL

Humus makers are bulky organic materials which are attacked by bacteria — these tiny organisms produce heat and also true humus, a magical material which cements clay or sand particles together to form soil crumbs.

Adding one or more humus makers is the only way you can transform your poor quality soil into crumbly earth which is easy to work and capable of holding both water and nutrients. Not all humus makers, however, are equally effective in producing true humus.

Raw humus makers are fresh plant or animal materials which stimulate bacterial activity in the soil. Heat is produced and soil structure is improved, but roots can be damaged and a nitrogen fertilizer is needed. Examples are fresh horse manure, cow manure and grass clippings. Grass clippings are less root-damaging than fresh manure but it is better to compost them.

Matured humus makers are safer — the true humus has been formed by bacterial action before the material is put into the soil. Garden-made compost is an example and is nowadays the most widely-used humus maker. Never burn greenstuff which can be composted.

Fibrous materials act as sponges and open up the soil, but they create very little bacterial activity and so are poor humus makers. Peat is the prime example — a good choice if you plan to grow acid-hating plants but an expensive and inefficient one under ordinary circumstances.

A humus maker can be added to the soil in three ways. Bulky material is incorporated as a bottom-of-the-trench layer at digging time, as a mulch around growing plants in spring and as a surface dressing which is forked into the upper soil surface in autumn.

Animal manure

Garden compost

Grass clippings

Peat

DIGGING

Digging has numerous benefits. The upper soil layer is broken up and clods are exposed to the elements. Compost or manure can be incorporated, annual weeds are buried and the roots of perennial weeds are exposed. If the drainage is poor you may want to consider double digging — see The Garden Expert for details.

If the soil texture is reasonable then digging is not usually necessary — on very light soil it can do more harm than good. If you do decide to dig then remember that it is essential to put a layer of organic matter at the bottom of the trench before turning over the soil.

(1) Choose the right season — early winter for most soils and early spring for light land. Choose the right day — the ground should be moist but not waterlogged nor frozen

(2) Use the right equipment — a spade for general work or a fork if the soil is very heavy or stony. Carry a scraper and use it to keep the blade or prongs clean

(3) Dig out a trench about 25 cm wide and 1 spade spit deep. Transport the removed soil to the other end of the plot. You will need this soil to fill in the final trench

(4) Spread a layer of bulky organic material all along the bottom of the trench. As a guide, use a bucketful per 3 m of trench. A sprinkling of bone meal can be added

(5)
Drive the spade in vertically. Press (do not kick) down on the blade. This should be at right angles to the trench

(6)
The next cut should be parallel to the trench 15 - 20 cm behind the face. Do not take larger slices to save time

(7)
Pull steadily (do not jerk) on the handle so as to lever the soil on to the blade. Lift up the block of soil

(8)
With a flick of the wrist turn the earth into the trench in front — turn the spadeful right over to bury the weeds

CHOOSING CAREFULLY

It happens to all of us. We see a plant at the garden centre or in a catalogue which is just what we are looking for, but the description on the label makes it clear that the soil where it is to grow is clearly not suitable. We can make one or other of two mistakes. The first is to assume that the planting advice is far too restrictive, so we buy it anyway. The second one is that we try to change the conditions to suit the plant — this route can mean a lot of work and may not succeed. It is better to pick a plant which is known to be reliable in the soil where it will have to grow. The lists on these two pages give numerous examples.

ALKALINE SOIL

The trees and shrubs listed below can be expected to thrive in cultivated alkaline soil provided their other needs are met. They should also succeed in neutral soil, but will do less well or may fail when grown in acid soil.

AUCUBA	MAHONIA
BERBERIS	MALUS
BUDDLEIA	PHILADELPHUS
CEANOTHUS	PHLOMIS
CEDRUS	POTENTILLA
CHOISYA	PRUNUS
CISTUS	PYRACANTHA
COTONEASTER	PYRUS
CRATAEGUS	RHUS
CYTISUS	RIBES
DAPHNE	ROBINIA
DEUTZIA	ROMNEYA
ELAEAGNUS	RUBUS
ESCALLONIA	SAMBUCUS
EUONYMUS	SANTOLINA
FORSYTHIA	SENECIO
FRAXINUS	SPARTIUM
FUCHSIA	SPIRAEA
HEBE	SYRINGA
HYPERICUM	TAMARIX
JUNIPERUS	ULEX
KERRIA	VIBURNUM
LABURNUM	WEIGELA

Hebe 'Autumn Glory'

Romneya coulteri

ACID SOIL

The trees and shrubs listed below can be expected to thrive in cultivated acid soil provided their other needs are met. Some will also succeed in neutral soil, but nearly all will do less well or may fail when grown in alkaline soil.

ABIES	KOELREUTERIA
AZALEA	LEUCOTHOE
CALLUNA	MAGNOLIA
CAMELLIA	PERNETTYA
CORYLOPSIS	PICEA
DABOECIA	PIERIS
DESFONTAINIA	RHODODENDRON
ENKIANTHUS	SARCOCOCCA
FOTHERGILLA	SKIMMIA
GAULTHERIA	TAXODIUM
HAMAMELIS	TSUGA
KALMIA	VACCINIUM

Kalmia latifolia

Rhododendron 'Glowing Embers'

BADLY-DRAINED SOIL

The plants listed below can be expected to thrive in soil which is permanently moist provided their other needs are met. Some may succeed in other soils, but will do less well or will fail in free-draining soil.

ALNUS	GUNNERA
ARUNCUS	LIGULARIA
ASTILBE	RHEUM
CALTHA	TAXODIUM
FILIPENDULA	TROLLIUS

HEAVY SOIL

The trees and shrubs listed below can be expected to thrive in cultivated clay-rich soil provided their other needs are met. They should also succeed in loamy soil, but may do less well when grown in light sandy soil.

ABELIA	MAHONIA
ABIES	MALUS
ACER	OSMANTHUS
AESCULUS	PHILADELPHUS
AUCUBA	PLATANUS
BERBERIS	POTENTILLA
BETULA	PRUNUS
CHAENOMELES	PYRACANTHA
CHOISYA	PYRUS
CORNUS	QUERCUS
CORYLUS	RIBES
COTONEASTER	ROSA
CRATAEGUS	RUBUS
CRYPTOMERIA	SALIX
EUCALYPTUS	SKIMMIA
FRAXINUS	SORBUS
HAMAMELIS	SPIRAEA
HEDERA	SYRINGA
HYPERICUM	TAXUS
ILEX	TILIA
KERRIA	VIBURNUM
LABURNUM	VINCA
MAGNOLIA	WEIGELA

LIGHT SOIL

The trees and shrubs listed below can be expected to thrive in cultivated light sandy soil provided their other needs are met. They should also succeed in loamy soil, but may do less well or fail when grown in heavy clayey soil.

AILANTHUS	KOELREUTERIA
AMELANCHIER	KOLKWITZIA
BUDDLEIA	LAVANDULA
BUXUS	PEROVSKIA
CASTANEA	PHLOMIS
CEDRUS	PHORMIUM
CERATOSTIGMA	PINUS
CISTUS	RHUS
CONVOLVULUS	ROBINIA
CORONILLA	ROMNEYA
CORTADERIA	ROSMARINUS
CUPRESSUS	SALVIA
CYTISUS	SAMBUCUS
ELAEAGNUS	SEDUM
ERICA	SENECIO
ERYNGIUM	SOLANUM
EUPHORBIA	SPARTIUM
GENISTA	SPIRAEA
GLEDITSIA	STEPHANANDRA
HELICHRYSUM	SYMPHORICARPOS
HIBISCUS	TAMARIX
HIPPOPHAE	ULEX
JUNIPERUS	YUCCA

Mahonia aquifolium

Ceratostigma wilmottianum

Coronilla glauca 'Variegata'

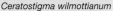

Viburnum davidii

Berberis darwinii

Convolvulus cneorum

MULCHING

Mulching is one of the most important ways of improving both the quality and appearance of your soil. It need cost you nothing and it is simple to do, and yet it is usually neglected. Basically a humus mulch is a layer of bulky organic matter placed around plants to improve soil structure and plant growth as well as to suppress weed growth. The standard time for applying a humus mulch is May when the soil is warm and moist. Remove debris and annual weeds before spreading a 5 - 7.5 cm thick layer of the chosen material around the stems and over bare ground. If material is short, place a 1 - 1.5 m wide ring around each tree and shrub.

WHAT IT DOES

The soil below is kept moist in summer, reducing the need to water. It is also kept cooler than soil without a mulch, and this moist and cool root zone promotes more active growth than in unmulched areas.

The soil is kept warmer than uncovered ground in winter — a definite benefit for many plants.

Some pests and diseases are kept in check. Obviously root flies are deterred and so are moles. U.S research indicates that eelworm numbers are reduced.

Some mulches such as well-rotted manure and garden compost do provide a small amount of plant food, but this is not enough to meet the needs of most plants, so some extra feeding may be needed.

Soil structure is improved for a number of reasons. Humus is added, earthworm activity is increased and soil capping by rain or watering is eliminated.

Vegetables are protected from rain splashes bouncing off the soil — a much ignored problem.

Annual weed growth is suppressed — those which break through are easily removed by hand pulling and so there is no need to hoe. Vigorous perennial weeds will be able to break through — consider a weed control mulch (page 63) if they are a serious problem.

WHAT TO USE

Peat

Used on both mixed borders and shrubberies. Widely available with a natural look, but when dry it tends to blow about or forms a cake which is difficult to wet. Does not produce true humus — not a good choice.

Well-rotted manure

Less attractive than peat or bark, but it is available very cheaply at farm or stable gate and is the best soil improver of all. Quality from an unknown source can be a problem — weed seeds may be present.

Bark or Cocoa shell

Bark is a better choice than peat. The chips should be 1 - 5 cm long. Cocoa shell is a good alternative but can be smelly when wet. Use in the same way as peat — reasonably attractive around trees and shrubs.

Garden compost

Free, and it gets rid of grass clippings, soft cuttings, old stems etc. Like manure it provides some nutrients and improves soil structure, but it is usually less effective. Poorly-made compost may be full of weeds.

Straw

Easy and cheap to obtain in rural areas where it is used in grand estates and tiny allotments, but it is rather unsightly in the front garden. Weed seeds may be present — a nitrogen rich fertilizer is necessary.

Leaf mould

Fallen leaves should not be wasted. Gather them up, moisten if necessary and squash into large black plastic bags and tie the top tightly. Black, crumbly leaf mould will be ready in 1 - 2 years.

Old growing compost

Spent growing compost has the virtues and limitations of peat with the added value of some nutrients. Examples include growing bags after use and spent mushroom compost.

Grass clippings

Short clippings from the lawn can be used as a shallow mulch (maximum height 2.5 cm) — keep away from the crowns of the plants. Top up as necessary in early summer. Do not use if lawn was weedy.

FEEDING

There are two basic reasons why soil may fail to support satisfactory growth. Firstly the soil structure may be poor — too much sand or clay with too little organic matter for proper crumb formation. The answer is to incorporate a bulky humus maker — see page 75. The other reason for poor performance is the shortage of one or more of the nutrients vital for plant growth. The addition of compost, manure etc will help a little, but the real answer is to use a fertilizer. A fertilizer is a material which provides appreciable quantities of one or more plant nutrients without adding significantly to the humus content of the soil.

WHAT TO USE

Quick-acting fertilizers

These types go to work almost at once, providing plants with a boost. Unfortunately most are not long-lasting. Nearly all the top-selling types belong here, the liquid and soluble powder ones, the proprietary powders and granules for roses, tomatoes etc, the general-purpose granular ones like Growmore and the 'straight' inorganic ones such as sulphate of ammonia.

Slow-acting fertilizers

These types have to break down before going to work, so speed of nutrient release depends on soil conditions. They go on working for longer than the quick-acting ones and are less likely to cause scorch, but do not expect a quick greening-up of the foliage. They are usually organic (hoof & horn, fish meal, bone meal etc) but may be mineral (for example rock phosphate).

Organic or Chemical?

At the plant root level the form of the nitrogen, phosphates and potash which enters is identical. However, some users of plant- and animal-based fertilizers such as dried poultry manure feel that these products have special virtues over chemical ones. Unfortunately the range of these organics is limited and they are generally more expensive than the popular chemical or 'artificial' fertilizers.

Steady-release fertilizers

A post-war development which is widely used by nurserymen for their container-grown plants and is also available to gardeners. A granular fertilizer is coated with a resin and this outer covering breaks down steadily in the soil. The nutrients are thus made available over a prolonged period — usually for 6 months. Spread around trees, shrubs or perennials in the spring.

WHAT TO FEED

You can have a soil analysis carried out, but it is more usual to take action on the basis of plant type, soil type, season of the year and the appearance of the plants. In order of fertilizer needs, vigorous container plants in unfed compost come top of the list followed by heavy-cropping vegetables, bedding plants, lawns and large-flowered perennials. Bottom of the list are well-established trees and shrubs. Soil type is important — sandy soils are hungry, especially in rainy areas. The best nutrient balance depends on the type of plant — see below.

THE FEEDING PROGRAMME

There are a few basic principles but there is no standard feeding programme. The traditional routine is to use a granular balanced fertilizer to enrich the soil before planting or to apply it around growing established shrubs and perennials at the start of the growing season. In late spring and summer a quick-acting liquid fertilizer is used — you will find a range of brands at your local garden centre. There are areas of the garden which are usually fed with a specific rather than a general fertilizer — the lawn, rose bed and tomato growing bag.

BALANCED N P_2O_5 K_2O	Nitrogen (N) content similar to Potash (K_2O)	Use as a general-purpose fertilizer for base feeding or as an in-season top dressing
HIGH N N P_2O_5 K_2O	Nitrogen (N) content higher than Potash (K_2O)	Use on grass, leaf vegetables and root-bound plants to boost growth and improve leaf colour
HIGH K_2O N P_2O_5 K_2O	Nitrogen (N) content lower than Potash (K_2O)	Use on fruit, flowers and potatoes to help flower quality and to increase crop yields

" THE GARDEN IS BROWN AFTER THE DROUGHT "

A dry spell becomes a drought when no reasonable rain has fallen for 14 days. This change of name has little significance for the gardener — a light sprinkling of rain during the dry fortnight stops it being a drought, but it makes hardly any difference to the garden.

The gardener's drought is a prolonged dry and warm or hot spell when there has been no worthwhile rain for weeks and the soil water reserves are low. If your garden is small and you have the time and equipment to water properly then your lawn and plants may not suffer, but it is a different story for most people. When the garden is large and/or there is a hosepipe ban the signs of drought will clearly and quite quickly appear. The first sign is that the young leaves of susceptible plants (newly-planted shrubs, bedding plants etc) start to look dull. Wilting is the next stage and pale brown areas appear on the lawn. Leaves start to shrivel and turn brown — leaf fall and/or plant collapse is the final stage if the drought period has been exceptionally prolonged. Plants do not have to reach this final stage before they are seriously harmed. Wilting of soft-stemmed plants is generally reversible — copious watering restores leaves and stems to their former healthy state. But wilting and browning of the leaves of woody evergreens can mean bare stems even when the rains arrive.

Of course there will be work to do to revive the garden once the rain returns, and you will find some advice on page 84. But there is also a great deal you can do to make sure that your garden will not suffer to the same extent in future years. Some of this work should be done before the dry weather arrives (page 81) and the rest of the anti-drought procedures are outlined on pages 82 - 83.

Making a Dry Garden

The dry or gravel garden is a feature of sub-tropical areas which have long, dry summers. In most areas of this country the sole purpose of a dry garden is to provide a decorative feature with an exotic appearance. There is an exception — in areas with low rainfall and sandy soil, such as East Anglia, it can also serve as a green oasis in the all-too-frequent hot and dry summers.

Cover the plot with woven polypropylene sheeting and plant through slits cut in the plastic — see page 63 for instructions. Choose bold architectural plants such as Yucca, Phormium, Cordyline, Tracheocarpus, ornamental grasses and bright drought-tolerant flowers such as Eschscholzia or Verbascum. Make sure that the plants are set further apart than usual. After planting cover the whole surface with gravel.

TAKING ACTION BEFORE A DROUGHT

If your garden begins to suffer quickly in dry weather it is worth taking action to reduce the chore of watering and the disappointment of losing plants. Do not wait until the drought arrives — there are jobs to do while the soil is still moist. The steps below will cut down the need for watering and there is a bonus — some of the work will improve plant growth and keep down weeds. Finally, buy watering equipment before the dry weather starts.

PLANTING FOR DROUGHT RESISTANCE

Step 1

Plants look lovely at the garden centre in summer, but wait until autumn if you can when the dry season is over. Before planting build up the water-holding capacity of the soil by forking or digging in plenty of humus-making material such as compost or manure — see page 75 for details. Try to choose low-risk plants if the site will be difficult or impossible to water.

Step 2

The water reservoir in the soil should be reasonably full before you begin sowing or planting. This calls for watering thoroughly if the soil is dry — the ground should be moist to a depth of about 20 cm. Now you are ready to start planting — use an organic-rich planting mixture as described on page 15. Water gently but thoroughly to settle the soil around the roots.

Step 3

With large plants it is a good idea to create a water catchment area for any future watering which may be necessary. With shrubs and trees build a ridge of soil around the base to create a watering basin. With large herbaceous plants such as dahlias or tomatoes you can bury a large plant pot at planting time near to the base of the stem.

Step 4

Mulching is the final step — a vital but underused technique which will increase the plant's ability to withstand drought. An organic layer of compost, well-rotted manure, bark chippings etc is placed around the base of the plant when the soil is moist and reasonably warm. Top up if necessary each year. See page 78 for details.

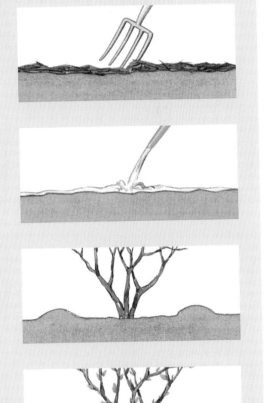

ADDITIONAL TIPS FOR DROUGHT RESISTANCE

- Use large containers. To avoid very frequent watering the pot or tub should be at least 25 cm deep. A leafy shrub or tree needs a container which is at least 45 cm wide and 30 cm deep.
- Pick fruit and vegetables shortly before going away if you plan a long summer holiday.
- Choose self-watering hanging baskets rather than moss-lined wire or plastic ones.

- Vegetables grown by the bed system withstand dry conditions better than plants in a traditional long-row plot.
- Windbreaks and light shade reduce water loss, but ground under trees or near hedges dries out quickly — the roots below are the cause.
- As a general rule plants with silvery or grey leaves have good drought resistance.

TAKING ACTION DURING A DROUGHT

The way most people treat their plants during a prolonged dry spell is wrong. Not only is it hard work but it can often do more harm than good. At first we do nothing and then spring into action when plants wilt. The lawn sprinkler is switched on for a short time every other day and the garden is dampened down on a daily basis with a watering can or hose. Read below to learn how to water properly.

WATER PROPERLY

The two golden rules

Never wait until the plants are showing serious signs of distress during a prolonged dry period. Wilting means you have waited too late — the time to start watering is when the foliage looks dull and the soil at a depth of 10 cm is dry.

•

Never apply a small amount of water (less than 5 litres per m) and then repeat the watering every few days. This constant soaking of the surface and water-starvation of the lower zone leads to rapid evaporation, surface rooting which is damaged in hot weather, and germination of weed seeds. Water in the right way. It is not just a matter of turning on a hose pipe until the ground is wet — see the steps below.

Step 1

Choose between overall watering and point watering. If you have large areas to cover and many plants of various sizes, overall watering must be your choice. This involves watering an area rather than restricting the water to the root zone of each individual plant. Some people use a watering can, but you really do need a hose pipe if watering is not to be a prolonged chore. The usual procedure is to walk along borders and around beds with a hand-held hose and suitable nozzle. A sprinkler makes the job easier and is essential for all but the tiniest lawn. Perhaps the best methods for watering vegetables are the seep hose and leaky pipe — see page 83. Point watering is used where there is a limited number of large plants to deal with — the methods used are designed to restrict the water to the immediate zone covered by the roots of each plant. You can either bury a large plant pot or build up a ridge of soil around the plant and fill with the required amount of water. Alternatively you can hold the hose over the earth around each plant.

Step 2

Water thoroughly and carefully. If you are using a watering can remove the rose unless you are watering seedlings or bedding plants. Hold the spout or hose nozzle close to the ground and water slowly around the plant — do not direct the water at the base of the plant and never use a powerful jet. If you use a sprinkler water in the evening — not in hot sunshine. With point watering apply 5 - 20 litres per plant, depending on the size of the plant, soil type and air temperature. With overall watering apply 10 - 20 litres per sq.m.

Step 3

Repeat the watering if rain does not fall. It may be necessary to repeat the watering if rain does not fall — do not assume that a light summer shower will top up the water reserves in the soil. There is no easy way to determine the right time for this repeat watering. Dig down with a trowel and examine the soil at 10 - 15 cm below the surface — it is time to water if it is dry. As a general rule watering is required every 5 - 7 days during a period of drought in summer — do not water every couple of days because the plants continue to droop or are not growing.

Watering the lawn

During a period of drought there is at first a loss of springiness in the turf and a general dullness over the surface. Later on the grass turns straw-coloured and unsightly. Before this stage you should have increased cutting height and the interval between mowings, and you will have to choose between two courses of action. First, you can decide to leave it to nature. Lawn grasses are very rarely killed by drought and recover quite quickly once the rains return. Watering is the alternative course of action, but it must be thorough. This calls for applying at least 20 litres per sq.m once a week until the dry spell ends. Do not use a hose pipe propped on the handle of a spade — water with a sprinkler so that a large area is covered. Do not try to take a middle course of action by sprinkling every few days to dampen the surface — this may do more harm than good.

WATERING EQUIPMENT

Watering can
Vital for point watering a few plants but quite impractical for overall watering in anything larger than a tiny garden. The standard size for general use is a 10 litre can fitted with a metal rose for small plants

Seep hose
Basically a plastic hose pipe with a series of pinholes along the sides. Plants are situated close to these holes — the water seeps through the holes to water the ground around the roots

Hose pipe
The usual type is made of PVC and is available in 15 m and 30 m lengths. Double-wall tubing is recommended. Use a reel for storage when not in use. Lay-flat tubing is wound into a cassette-like case for easy storage

Leaky pipe
An advance on the seep hose. The hose pipe is porous so that water seeps out along its whole length — plants are not set at any particular point. Buy in kit form — bury several centimetres below the soil surface

Sprinkler
The simplest type of sprinkler system. The pattern is quite even but the area covered is relatively small, so a series of these fixed watering points is necessary to water a bed or border. Improved types are available

WATER THE HIGH-RISK PLANTS & AREAS PROPERLY & PROMPTLY

The plants and areas below are at greater risk than average during dry weather.

- **Bedding plants** for at least 6 weeks after planting. Even when established, shallow rooting means that they remain at risk
- **Hardy perennials** for the first year after planting
- **Shrubs** and **trees** for the first 1 - 2 years after planting. Generally, mature trees and shrubs are less at risk than other plants
- Numerous **vegetables** — tomatoes, cucumbers, sweet corn, beans, peas, onions, marrows and celery
- Several **soft fruits** — strawberries and currants

- **Containers** — tubs, hanging baskets, window boxes, growing bags etc. Plants in containers are at the top of the risk list
- **Sandy** and **low-humus** soils
- **Shallow-rooted plants.** Not all of these plants are small — some (e.g Hydrangea, silver birch, Rhododendron etc) are large shrubs or trees
- **Rain-shadow plants** — specimens growing within 60 cm of the house wall
- **Underplanting** — most plants growing under hedges and trees
- **Fruit trees** when the fruit begins to swell

WATER THE LOW-RISK PLANTS IF THEY START TO SUFFER

The plants below are at less risk than the average for others in their group (e.g bedding plants, shrubs) during dry weather.

ABELIA	COREOPSIS	GAILLARDIA	LAVANDULA	SEDUM
ACANTHUS	COSMOS	GAZANIA	LIATRIS	SEMPERVIVUM
ACHILLEA	COTINUS	GENISTA	MAHONIA	SENECIO
ALYSSUM	COTONEASTER	GERANIUM	NEPETA	STACHYS
ARMERIA	CYTISUS	GRASSES	OENOTHERA	TAMARIX
ARTEMISIA	DIANTHUS	HELIANTHEMUM	PACHYSANDRA	THYMUS
BUDDLEIA	ERYNGIUM	HELICHRYSUM	PEROVSKIA	WALDSTEINIA
CEANOTHUS	EUONYMUS	HIBISCUS	PHORMIUM	WEIGELA
CISTUS	EUPHORBIA	IBERIS	PYRACANTHA	YUCCA
CONVOLVULUS	FELICIA	IPOMOEA	ROSMARINUS	ZINNIA

TAKING ACTION AFTER A DROUGHT

The rain has returned and the ground has been soaked. A green haze has begun to appear on the brown areas on the lawn and some of the wilted plants are now back to normal. But overall the garden is unsightly and worrying — if you have not been able to water then there will be a patchy lawn, premature leaf fall and some plants may be beyond saving. Obviously you want to take some action, but it is wise to read the sections below before reaching for the secateurs and lawn mower.

LAWN

Unless the lawn is reasonably small and/or is in front of the house you will probably have left it alone and waited for rain. With continued dry weather brown patches will have developed and these may have spread to cover the whole area. Now that rain has fallen the grass has started to grow again as promised, but the mottled appearance will stay for some time and drought-resistant weeds such as yarrow and clover could have spread rapidly. The golden rule is to do nothing at first and then mow with the cutter raised to about 5 cm for the rest of the season. Don't rake or feed the lawn, and keep off the patches which are still brown. The time to start work is in the spring — see the Lawn Renovation Programme on page 12.

TREES & SHRUBS

Established trees and large shrubs are the plants most likely to be unaffected by a long period of dry weather as their roots penetrate deep down into the ground. However, if the root zone does become dry then the effect can be very serious or fatal. Leaf rolling, leaf browning and leaf fall are the worrying signs — they are most likely to occur with newly-planted specimens and shallow-rooted types like Camellia, Hydrangea, Rhododendron and Heathers. With badly affected plants carry out Renewal Pruning — see pages 40 - 46.

SOIL

Cracks in the soil mean that the clay content is high and the organic content is low. These cracks are not only unsightly — they can damage tree and shrub roots. They are a clear indication that the soil needs to be improved. The two-stage plan should be to incorporate a 5 cm layer of humus-making material (old manure, leaf mould, compost etc) into the soil by digging or forking in and then laying down a mulch in late spring.

FLOWERS

Cut back damaged perennials to where the stems seem to be green and healthy — new growth should take place now that the ground has been moistened by the rain. Bedding plants need the same treatment — there could be a late flush of flowers in a few weeks time. If your beds and borders have suffered badly despite watering then remember to mulch around the plants next year. In addition you may have not been watering properly — read the advice on page 82. Cut back all brown stems and leaves and water thoroughly — don't rely on rain alone. If possible stand pots in a tray or bowl of water until the compost surface is wet.

" THE BORDERS ARE NOW SO SHADY "

You are unhappy with the shady parts of your garden because the plants growing there are doing badly. The roses, bedding plants and so on look fine elsewhere, but in the shade under trees the stems are leggy and the floral display is disappointing.

There are several reasons why you have now decided to do something about it. You may have just moved house and you have no intention of living with the disappointing display your predecessor seemed to accept. Another reason may be that you have put up with the problem for years and have decided to try to have a brighter bed or border despite the shade problem. Finally it may be a new problem, and this happens in millions of gardens. Formerly the plants in the bed or border were unaffected by the newly-planted trees or hedge, but now that these introductions have grown into large specimens the flowers and shrubs below have started to suffer.

Something has to be done, but don't rush for a saw just yet. Trees in keeping with the size of your garden are vital to provide height and a sense of maturity. Pruning back may well be necessary, but felling is a step which needs very careful consideration. The dappled shade from the leaves and branches can be an attractive feature — the secret is to grow plants which thrive under these conditions. There are shade-tolerant trees, shrubs, border perennials and annuals — it's just a matter of making the right choice and the lists later in this section should help you.

A final word about the future. When choosing a new tree or large shrub do check on the anticipated height after 10 years. The same applies to buying vigorous hedging plants — think about the future problem you may be creating for the existing plants in the garden.

SOLVING THE PROBLEM

GROW SHADE-TOLERANT PLANTS (pages 86 - 87)	or	REMOVE OR REDUCE THE CAUSE OF THE SHADE (page 88)	or	REMOVE THE PLANTS (page 88)

Alternative 1:
GROW SHADE-TOLERANT PLANTS

A basic mistake is trying to grow 'ordinary' plants in a shady situation. Many plants will disappoint or may actually fail if subjected to shade for much of the day, but there are a large number of plants which will flourish under these conditions. Another mistake is to assume that all shade-loving plants are dull. Foliage plants are important where light is scarce, but there are many with interesting shapes. In addition there are variegated types with white or yellow edges or patches on the leaves which do better away from the glare of day-long bright light. There is also a wide range of flowering types — the lists on these pages should help you to bring both colour and interest to the darker parts of your garden.

Using the beauty of shade

Shade can be used to your advantage — it is one of the design features of the garden. Not too much, of course, but not too little. The contrast of well-lit areas with darker areas and shadows can create a delightful picture as in the photograph above.

Using leaf colour

Your prime objective is to brighten up the area in shade — do not underrate the value of foliage towards this end. Flowers are fine, but the display is often short-lived. Colourful foliage lasts all season long — with evergreens it lasts all year. In the border above there are greens, yellows and reds from Euonymus, Heuchera, ferns and Hosta.

Looking after the plants under trees

Choosing suitable varieties is only half the story. Plants in this situation have extra hardships to face apart from light shortage. Dryness at the roots can be a serious problem — the tree roots are a drain on the soil's moisture reserves below the plants and the canopy of foliage partly stops water reaching the plants from above. In addition the tree roots may deplete the nutrient content of the soil. All this means that a poor showing under trees may be due to water and nutrient shortage and not just light shortage. Tackle the problem by sprinkling a balanced fertilizer around the plants in early spring, applying a mulch in late spring and watering thoroughly during dry spells in summer.

Covering a shady wall

The number of plants which will thrive on a north-facing wall or solid fence is limited — tried and tested ones are listed below. The area immediately next to the wall is often dry because it is in a rain shadow — always leave at least 30 cm between the plant and the stone, brick or wood.

Hydrangea petiolaris • Lonicera japonica

Hedera spp • Polygonum baldschuanicum

Clematis montana • Parthenocissus spp

Jasminum nudiflorum • Akebia quinata

Choosing suitable plants

NAME	HEIGHT
Aconitum orientale	1.2 m
Ajuga reptans	15 cm
Alchemilla mollis	50 cm
Anemone blanda	20 cm
Aucuba japonica	1.5 m
Bergenia cordifolia	45 cm
Brunnera macrophylla	40 cm
Buxus sempervirens	2 m
Camellia japonica	1.5 m
Convallaria majalis	20 cm
Cotoneaster horizontalis	60 cm
Crataegus spp	3 m
Cyclamen hederifolium	10 cm
Danae racemosa	1 m
Daphne odora	1 m
Digitalis spp	60 cm - 1.5 m
Epimedium perralchicum	50 cm
Euonymus fortunei	1 m
Euphorbia spp	30 cm - 1.5 m
Fatsia japonica	2 m
Ferns	10 cm - 1 m
Geranium endressii	60 cm
Geranium macrorrhizum	30 cm
Helleborus foetidus	45 cm

NAME	HEIGHT
Hosta spp	60 cm
Hypericum calycinum	45 cm
Ilex aquifolium	5 m
Iris foetidissima	50 cm
Lamium galeobdolon	30 cm
Ligustrum japonicum	2 m
Liriope muscari	30 cm
Mahonia spp	30 cm - 2 m
Osmanthus burkwoodii	1.8 m
Pachysandra terminalis	20 cm
Pieris spp	1 - 2 m
Polygonatum multiflorum	50 cm
Prunus laurocerasus	4 m
Pulmonaria officinalis	30 cm
Rhododendron spp	30 cm - 5 m
Rubus odoratus	2 m
Ruscus aculeatus	1 m
Sarcococca hookeriana	1 m
Skimmia spp	1 m
Sorbus aucuparia	3 - 5 m
Symphoricarpos albus	2 m
Viburnum davidii	1.5 m
Vinca spp	15 - 30 cm
Waldsteinia ternata	10 cm

Hosta sieboldiana 'Elegans'

Pieris formosa forrestii

Anemone blanda

Ajuga reptans

Vinca minor 'Gertrude Jekyll'

Alternative 2:
REMOVE OR REDUCE THE CAUSE OF THE SHADE

Most causes of shade are permanent features which are beyond our control. The house, fences, sheds, nearby buildings, garage etc are there to stay. Trees are different as they are not necessarily permanent, and so they are the shade-makers we can consider for removal. As stated in the introduction tree felling should never be undertaken lightly, but thinning of an overgrown shrubbery is certainly worth considering. The tall and stately tree in the corner of the front garden may be the cause of the problem but it obviously has to stay. However, if the shade it casts has only recently reduced the display of the plants below then renewal pruning can be the answer. A combination of crown lifting and crown reducing (see page 39) will certainly let in more light and if the tree can be pollarded (page 39) then the problem is removed. Conifers can be more difficult to deal with — the small plant you bought from the garden centre can quickly become a shade-casting monster if you made the wrong choice. The usual advice is to remove an over-large specimen and replace it with a more restrained variety if shade is a serious problem. You can try trimming it back to form a smaller conical shape, but few conifers respond well to pruning. Hedges can be an even more difficult problem as denseness must be kept to ensure privacy. Top and trim them regularly, but growing shade-loving varieties below them is the most acceptable answer to a shade problem.

Alternative 3:
REMOVE THE PLANTS

Getting rid of the plants and covering the area with paving, gravel or decking seems a drastic way of solving the shade problem and is certainly not recommended in the large majority of cases. TV makeover programmes have stimulated interest in covering an increasing part of the garden with hard landscaping of this sort, but this is often regrettable when the bed or border is flourishing. The better answer for shade is to reduce the cause if you can or to plant with shade-tolerant or shade-loving varieties. There is, however, one situation where it is worth considering getting rid of the greenery. Maintaining a lawn under a tree which bears a dense canopy of leaves is extremely difficult. Food and water shortage combined with shade exhausts the grasses and the drip from the edge of the leaf canopy is damaging. The usual result is sparse turf and abundant moss. Lawn removal in the affected area is the only long-term answer — you can use the land for shade-lovers and bulbs, but an alternative idea is to pave the area. There can be a similar problem with a tiny lawn in a densely-shaded courtyard or garden corner. If the grass here is a constant disappointment it may be better to create a paved or gravel area on which you can have seats, a range of pots etc.

CHAPTER 4

DESIGN BASICS

Up to now this book has dealt with garden renewal by working on or replacing individual or groups of plants, and also the way you can improve certain features such as the rockery or pond.

That may not be enough for you. You may feel that the garden needs a complete overhaul or that some of the key features should be changed. At this point we enter the world of garden design. This chapter sets out the basics of the subject — the types of designs which are available and the steps you should take to transform all or part of your property into a garden which will give you pleasure.

This chapter is not a boiled-down version of a traditional garden design book. There are not pages and pages of garden plans and planting lists — these are readily available in gardening magazines and books you can borrow from the library. Best of all you can walk around your area and see the sort of style which appeals to you as well as the plants which grow well locally. The purpose of this chapter is to explain the various steps you must take in order to move from a feeling of dissatisfaction with your present plot to a garden which delights you.

At the outset you must realise that a 'good' design does not exist as a matter of fact — it is a matter of opinion. From your standpoint there are five elements which make up good design:

- The garden must appeal strongly to you and your family.

- The garden must be labour-saving unless you have lots of time to spare

or lots of money to pay someone to do the work for you.

- The garden must not cost more to create or maintain than you can afford.

- The garden must provide a suitable home for the plants you have chosen so that they can thrive.

- The garden must not be truly objectionable to the people who are likely to call. That will include friends, relatives and neighbours.

It may be that you want to make major changes because the garden is overgrown with a jungle of poorly-performing shrubs and perennials. But how did the garden look before it got out of hand? If a few years ago the essential five elements described above were present then think again. It may be better to leave the basic structure alone and concentrate on renewal pruning and replanting.

Major changes may be necessary, and in that case you should plan properly before taking any action in the garden. If you have moved house during late autumn or winter then it is a good idea to see what you have before digging up beds and borders. There may be bulbs and border plants to surprise you in the spring and summer, and some or all of them may be worth retaining. In your own long-established garden you can begin to make your plans straight away — work steadily from Step 1 to Step 8. Then you will be ready to go outside and start work on your new garden — this is Step 9 on page 125.

STEP 1 CHOOSE A STYLE

If you have recently moved house this step may well be vital. The garden you have inherited may be hopelessly overgrown or it may have no appeal for you — this is the time to consider whether a change of style or a variation of the existing style would be a good idea.

No garden designer has been clever enough (or perhaps foolish enough) to try to establish a universally-acceptable classification of clear-cut styles for the home gardener. The types on the following pages are the ones you are most likely to see, but you will find different lists in other books. The key point is that you should not decide on any style, whatever it happens to be called, until you have answered two vital questions — what have I got and what do I want?

Take your time in filling out the questionnaire below and carefully consider your answers. Then look through the styles in this section — your notes should help you find the one that is right for both you and your situation, provided that it meets the five requirements on page 89. It may be that the present style is fine — there is just a need for a change in its design. Remember that the whole garden need not be given over to a single style — a wildflower bed or border can sit comfortably in an informal standard garden and an architectural area may not be out of place in a formal standard garden around a modern house.

What have I got?

SOIL TYPE
Loam/heavy/light/acid/alkaline — see p.74 for guidance

PLOT SIZE
Tiny/small/average/large/country estate

STYLE
Happy/unhappy with all/part of the present style

CHANGE NEEDED
Start from scratch/major changes/minor changes

MONEY AVAILABLE
Hard landscaping (walls, paving etc) is expensive

LABOUR AVAILABLE
Self/ self+helpers /professional help

LIGHT & SHADE
Open and sunny/enclosed and shady

What is important?

WORK
Somewhere to relax/ somewhere to work

PRIVACY
Privacy/open plan

STYLE
Traditional/modern/natural/off-beat design

PURPOSE
A garden for us/a garden to impress our friends

FAMILY
A place for children/pets

OUTDOOR LIVING
A place for entertaining/sitting/eating outdoors

FEATURES
Items which must be included — see pages 108-117

Town Garden

A town garden in a rural setting. Old-fashioned plants and subdued flower colours have been used so that the plot mirrors the verdant leafy surroundings — unity is a feature of good garden design (see page 101). Green pots rather than earthenware ones have been chosen

Paving is one of the dominant features of the town garden and so making the right choice is important. It need not be a sea of plain slabs — in this garden there is a mixture of gravel, reconstituted stone slabs, brick and natural stone to accompany but not overwhelm the planting

The expression 'town garden' has no precise meaning. Some designers use it to mean any small plot in an urban area irrespective of whether grass is grown or not. In this book 'town garden' describes a small plot where paving material is used instead of a lawn. The key feature is the absence of grass rather than the size of the garden.

The creation of an attractive urban garden faces a number of difficulties. On the average plot there are walls which cast considerable shade. Traffic noise can be a problem and so can air pollution from cars etc, and there can be a lack of privacy. Finally, tool storage and waste plant disposal can pose problems.

The town garden approach is the recommended one as a lawn under these conditions would be a disappointment, and the design must be a formal one — there is just no way of aiming for a natural look. Clothe the walls and/or fences where you can with plants to increase privacy and cut down traffic noise. Use borders/beds and containers for planting — a liberal use of evergreens and variegated small trees or shrubs is recommended to give year-round living colour. Achieve a dramatic effect by growing architectural plants (see page 69) wherever you can. Raised beds and small water features are excellent items for a town garden.

Town Garden trees & shrubs

Salix exigua
Pinus mugo 'Gnom'
Rosa rugosa
Camellia japonica
Fatsia japonica
Stachys lanata
Magnolia stellata
Viburnum tinus
Choisya ternata
Lonicera americana
Mahonia 'Charity'
Dryopteris filix-mas
Buxus sempervirens
Arundinaria murielae
Pieris 'Forest Flame'
Prunus 'Amanogawa'
Acer negundo 'Flamingo'
Skimmia japonica 'Rubella'
Hydrangea macrophylla
Hedera helix 'Goldheart'
Aucuba japonica 'Variegata'
Jasminum nudiflorum

Is this style right for you?

If your plot is small and enclosed then a lawn-free town garden would be a good choice, especially if you like sitting outdoors.

Standard Garden

The small standard garden. The back garden may be no wider than the house and here there is little scope for flowing lines and an informal look. In these small plots a formal design is usually chosen. Circles and straight lines need not be dull — see the next page for ways to add interest

The large standard garden. The back garden may extend for an acre or more and numerous features may be present — pool, rockery, arches etc. A popular approach is to have a formal design near the house and an informal style with a winding path and curved borders at the outer reaches

The standard style dominates the garden scene — mile after mile of these gardens can be seen from any railway carriage window. The front garden may be treated in several ways — grass is a common but by no means a general feature. It is the back garden which sets the style. There is a lawn which usually covers most of the area, and there is a selection of flowers, shrubs and/or trees to add colour and interest. At least one path or drive leads to the house and the property is totally or partly enclosed by a wall, fencing or hedge. These are the only features which all standard-style gardens have in common.

With no other features the garden could look dull. To add interest to your plot there are many optional extras — see the list on the right. Some should be included but don't overdo it. If you are changing your hackneyed standard-style garden then think about moving away from the central rectangular lawn and its frill of borders and scattering of beds. Consider curves and hidden areas — see pages 66 - 67. Consider the bed system for vegetables — see pages 24 - 25. If you want an easy-care garden read pages 56 - 60 before you begin.

Finally, remember that all of these points are suggestions — if your ideal is a green handkerchief with a flowery edging then that is a good design.

Essential features

- Lawn
- Beds and/or borders
- Paths and/or drives
- Fencing, walls and/or hedges

Optional extras

- Play area (Sand box etc)
- Paved area (Table, chairs etc)
- Water area (Pond etc)
- Utility area (Shed, compost bin etc)
- Greenhouse
- Pergola/Archway
- Rock garden
- Steps
- Barbeque
- Ornaments (Sundial, birdtable etc)
- Vegetable plot
- Herb garden
- Containers (Pots, tubs etc)
- Lighting

Is this style right for you?

If you want your back garden to keep its lawn with a selection of flowers and shrubs then this is the style for you. Depending on your skill it can be restfully plain or outstandingly vibrant.

The Formal Approach

In the strictly formal garden there is a central axis and the right-hand side is a mirror image of the left side. Paths are straight and the shapes of beds, borders, pools etc are geometrical — squares, rectangles, circles, ovals etc. Trimmed hedges to divide beds and provide privacy are often key features. There are many examples in our great gardens, but for most people this approach is too sterile and quite unsuitable for a family garden.

The modern-day formal garden still relies on geometrical shapes but the requirement for one side of the garden or garden area to be just like the other has gone. So has the idea that the plants should be naturally neat or should be kept trimmed to avoid an untidy look. One of the ways to enliven a formal garden is to interlock some of the geometric shapes — a circular bed cutting into a circular paved area or square flower beds linked into a rectangular paved area.

The Informal Approach

In the informal garden there is no feeling of a collection of geometrical patterns — here the plants and not the shapes are the key feature. Winding paths and irregularly-shaped beds and borders are key features, and so is the use of tall plants and structures to hide the boundaries from view. Curves are paramount, but keep them simple and avoid wavy and fussy shapes at all costs.

It may seem strange but designing a 'natural' looking garden is more difficult than drawing up plans for a strictly formal one. In the informal garden one has to try to get a sense of balance with objects which are quite different in size and shape. One large plant may call for a group of small ones nearby to provide balance.

Borders are usually wider than the narrow straight strips of the formal garden, and where width is limited it is usually better to have a single side border. Keep the centre open — beds in the centre of the lawn will make the garden look smaller.

The Basic Version

This is the back garden you will see everywhere — a square or rectangular plot with a central lawn and one or more borders at the edges. Bedding plants are in the flower beds and a mixture of plants is in the borders. There are few other features — the ones you are most likely to find are a vegetable plot at the bottom of the garden and containers close to the house. In most cases there is no call for change — the children play on the lawn, the beds provide a splash of colour, there is a place to sit in the sun and there are the vegetables to look after.

The De-luxe Version

Here the garden is more than a place for plants and most of the principles of good design have been incorporated. The use of formal and informal styles, hidden areas and clever use of focal points create what garden architects call 'tension' — a sudden increase in attention as you move from one part of the garden to the other. Materials are in keeping with the style of the house and there are adequate areas for sitting or entertaining. An important feature is the presence of year-round colour, and regular pruning and weeding ensure year-round admiration.

Country House Garden

The classical country house garden with a wrap-around lawn surrounding a large barn conversion. The plant beds are at some distance from the dwelling, and so are the outbuildings. The object here has been to give a feeling of open space around the house

The wrap-around lawn and a feeling of uncluttered space are not essential features of the country house garden. Deep borders and large beds surround this beautiful old manor house in East Anglia — here the lawns and not the flowers have been consigned to the outer reaches

The country house garden is usually found in a rural area, but they also occur in the suburbs. It is usually larger than the standard model, but not always. Trees and large shrubs always play a key role, but they may also do so in a standard plot. The basic difference is that a country house garden is a wrap-round plot which surrounds the house — there is no division into front and back garden. This means that here we have a single unit which offers great scope for creative landscaping.

There is often a touch of formal design close to the house (rectangular terrace, square flower beds flanking steps etc) and in the 'garden rooms' in the outer reaches of the garden (rose garden, box-edged knot garden, herb garden etc). The overall picture, however, is one of informal shapes and informal planting. The use of trees and large shrubs provides a woodland look and the main source of colour is traditionally a long and wide herbaceous border. Holding all the elements together is the large lawn with areas of less-manicured grassland in the large estate gardens.

There is great scope in the large wrap-round garden to have path-linked 'rooms' — a wildflower area, a mediterranean garden etc. The workaday regions (vegetable plot, compost heap etc) can be hidden away. Here we have the world's idea of a classic English garden.

Country Garden features

Extensive lawn (Buttercups and daisies are acceptable)

Stone, brick or gravel paths (Concrete is not acceptable)

Stone ornaments (Urns, statues, sundial etc)

Wood or wrought iron seats

Shrub roses and old-fashioned climbers

Herbaceous plants grown in groups rather than single specimens

Summerhouse

Winding walkways

Beds surrounded by clipped box hedging

Specimen trees

Boundary fencing hidden by shrubs, hedging etc

Rhododendrons and azaleas if soil is acid

Is this style right for you?

Yes, if the garden is large and wraps around the house. Can look out of place around a contemporary style property.

Cottage Garden

Plant clumps are large — perennials are not often divided. There is no planning — introductions are planted wherever there is room

Modern hard landscaping is avoided. Weathered pots, old sinks and low brick or stone walls form the framework

Paths are generally straight and made of brick, stone or compressed earth — modern surfaces should be avoided. Edges are hidden by flanking plants

For centuries the cottage garden was the standard style to be found around the small dwellings in every village in the land, but that time is past. The true cottage garden is now quite a rarity, but it is still a welcome sight as a reminder of our horticultural heritage.

There are a number of key features. The basic one is a complete lack of formality — plants are crowded together to form a jumble of colours, shapes and sizes. A second feature is the use of old-fashioned plants. Modern roses and half-hardy annuals creep in these days, but they do not belong in the true cottage garden.

Floral colour should come from perennials, self-sown annuals, bulbs and some flowering shrubs — in addition there will be shrub roses in the beds and rambler roses on the house walls. Fragrance is important, and so is a kaleidoscope of colours.

The cottage garden has always had to work for a living. Vegetables such as cabbage, broad beans and onions fill the spaces between the flowers. Herbs like rosemary, mint and sage are another essential ingredient.

In the old days nothing was bought — seeds were saved, cuttings were rooted and plants were exchanged with neighbours. Things have changed, but even today the cottage garden owner is not the garden centre's favourite customer.

Favourite Cottage Garden plants

Lavender
Rose
Honeysuckle
Hollyhock
Shasta Daisy
Sunflower
Catmint
Geranium
Clematis
Pinks
Chives
Love-in-a-mist
Nasturtium
Daylily
Phlox
Hellebores
Aquilegia
Achillea
Pyracantha
Cotoneaster
Canterbury Bells
Lupin
Red-hot Poker
Parsley

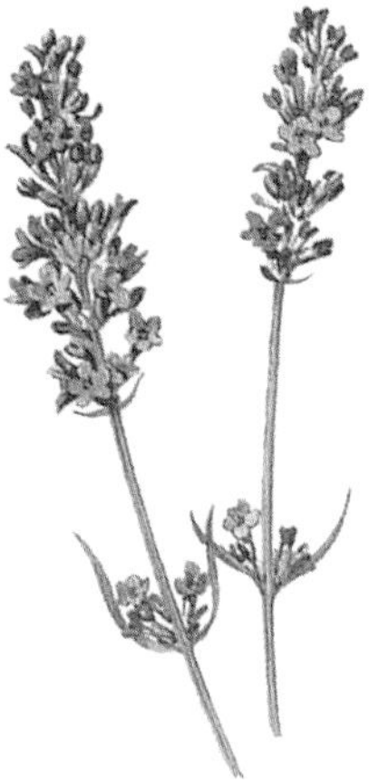

Is this style right for you?

This style is at home on a moderate-sized plot around a rural house. It is decidedly unhappy in a modern suburban setting.

Architectural Garden

Starkly simple. The hard landscape is colourless and the planting is plain — architectural plants have not been used. Not for everybody's taste, of course, but it is much more eye-catching than the paved front gardens which are now such a common sight. The stone balls and cubes are effective focal points

The other end of the scale from the example on the left. There is no white to be seen and the large Agaves are a vital part of the garden. A garden made to impress lovers of modern design and to horrify traditionalists who believe that gardens are a place for plants

In the architectural garden the designer sets out to produce a non-living structure which looks attractive in summer and winter, and into which plants are introduced to add living colour and living shapes. Here paths, walls and containers are chosen for their decorative and not simply their functional role. Trees and shrubs are chosen for their shape and leaf colours just as much as their blooms. Flowers, if present, are in formal beds, borders or containers.

There is a growing trend these days to convert small front plots into architectural gardens for the purely practical purpose of providing off-the-street parking for the car — unfortunately the result is so often devoid of any worthwhile planting. Much better examples are to be seen in wall-enclosed courtyard gardens where attractive paving, wall features, ironwork, flower-filled pots etc are blended together.

Treating a large back garden in this way can be stunning, but be warned. Not only will it be expensive to create but it can be a definite deterrent to a would-be buyer if you decide to move house. It may be wonderful as an outdoor living or dining area when furnished with lighting, gas heaters, tables, chairs etc, but it is a horror for the keen and active traditional gardener.

Plants for the Architectural Garden

Palms
Bamboos
Grasses
Ferns
Conifers
Yucca gloriosa
Canna indica
Viburnum davidii
Agave americana
Myrtus communis
Phormium tenax
Cynara cardunculus
Musa basjoo
Agapanthus africanus
Aralia elata variegata
Citrus mitis
Rhus typhina
Zantedeschia aethiopica
Acer palmatum
Robinia pseudoacacia
Kalmia latifolia

Is this style right for you ?

If this style really appeals to you then it is worth considering if the house is contemporary and you want an almost gardening-free life.

Wildflower Garden

This wildflower meadow provides a mass of colour in late spring — a reminder of the flower-filled fields of times gone by. Unfortunately weed grasses are a serious problem in most soils, and even when they are not present the area looks extremely dull when the flowers are absent

Clumps of wildflowers growing among rocks and/or native trees and shrubs are more appealing to many people than the wildflower meadow. Plant care is easier and the permanent residents of the plot provide some interest when the wildflower plants have died down

A wildflower garden seeks to look like an area of the countryside set next to your house — it may take up all of your property or just a section of it. The key feature is the flower-filled meadow planted with native species which produce their delicate, pastel-coloured blooms in spring and autumn. The design style is generally informal and its features should be in keeping — wattle fences, rural seating etc.

Creating a wildflower garden is not an easy option. First of all, it is necessary to remove the top 5 cm of soil as you need infertile soil for wild flowers. Kill re-emerging weeds and grasses with glyphosate before sowing with a wild flower mixture from your garden centre or specialist supplier — it is essential to choose a mix which is suitable for your soil type. On a small plot wildflower seedlings can be planted as an alternative to sowing seed.

Cutting takes place in July — trim down to about 10 cm and after a few weeks rake up the clippings. Never apply a fertilizer — in fertile soil the wildflowers may be quickly swamped by weeds such as couch grass and nettles.

A wild garden is not the same thing. It will contain a wildflower area, but its key feature is the provision of wildlife-attracting areas — nesting boxes, water, log piles, berry-bearing shrubs, native and cultivated plants which attract butterflies and so on.

Favourite wildflower species

White campion
Ragged robin
Betony
Crane's bill
Ox-eye daisy
Field poppy
Corncockle
Field scabious
Corn marigold
Meadow buttercup
Wild pansy
Musk mallow
Agrimony
Daffodil
Cat's ear
Primrose
Scentless mayweed
Bluebell
Vetch
Lily of the valley
Foxglove

Is this style right for you?

Yes, if you really want a natural look and accept that for much of the year it may not be attractive. Success is something of a gamble.

STEP 2

PREPARE A SITE PLAN

1: Begin with a rough sketch

Start with a large piece of paper on a clip board. Make a rough sketch plan of the house and the boundaries of your property — use a pencil and not a pen as even the experts have to rub out and make corrections at this survey stage. Within this plan mark the main features of the garden and outside the plan draw an arrow indicating north. The features should include more than the obvious things like beds, borders, paths, garden sheds etc. If the site is a new one mark deep hollows left by the builder, dead trees and so on — in an established garden mark poorly-drained areas, frost pockets etc if these are known.

Having drawn in the features, look out of the windows of the rooms in which you spend or plan to spend much of your time. See if there are any attractive views beyond your boundary and mark them on the sketch — you will not want to block these views when you draw up your design. Now look for eyesores and make a note of them. Almost every garden has an eyesore — the neighbour's dilapidated garden shed or compost heap, a nearby factory chimney etc. In your final design it will be necessary to screen out these areas if possible.

On the rough drawing write down the distances between the corners of the site by running the tape from one to the other. It is a good idea to use a red pen if you have drawn in lots of features and your sketch is crowded with pencil lines. For features within the garden you will sometimes have to use the process known as triangulation (see page 99) when preparing the site plan. This involves taking two measurements in order to fix the position of the feature — one from each side of the house or from two other fixtures. See the sketch below for examples.

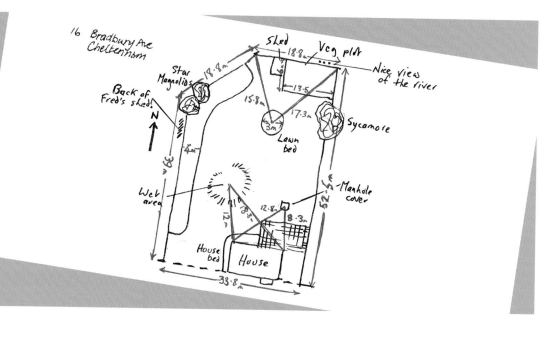

2: Draw the Site Plan

You are now ready to prepare a scale plan of your garden. Use graph paper and pick a scale which will allow the plan to fill most of the sheet — 1 : 50 and 1 : 100 are popular scales. Draw in the house to scale and then draw in each feature using the measurements noted on your rough sketch plan. Triangulation may be necessary — see below. Mark beds and borders in green, use a red pencil to show eyesores and a yellow one to highlight attractive vistas you wish to retain.

There is one more task. Pick a day when blue skies are forecast and in the morning mark the shaded area in blue on your plan. Repeat at noon and in the evening — the unshaded area is the 'full sun' zone.

Of course, Step 2 need only be carried out in full for a virgin site or where complete remodelling is planned. However, it is worthwhile even if only a minor change is intended. You will have a reference plan of your garden which can be used for future planning.

Triangulation

This technique will enable you to plot the in-garden features accurately on your site plan. Set the compasses to one of the distances marked on your rough sketch. Now place the point of the compasses on the relevant spot from which it was measured — the left hand corner of the house to fix the position of the manhole cover in the example on page 98. Draw an arc, and repeat the process from the second measuring point with the second distance — the right hand corner of the house in the rough sketch. Draw another arc, and the feature is at the point where the two arcs cross.

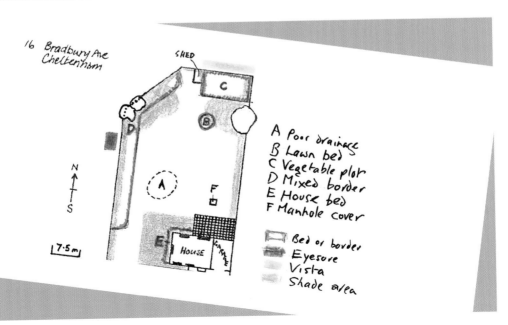

16 Bradbury Ave
Cheltenham

SHED

A Poor drainage
B Lawn bed
C Vegetable plot
D Mixed border
E House bed
F Manhole cover

Bed or border
Eyesore
Vista
Shade area

7·5 m

HOUSE

READ THE
GOOD DESIGN RULES

You will be doing nothing 'wrong' if you choose to ignore the advice on this page and the other tips up to page 103. The principles set out here are what the professionals regard as good design — they are ways to ensure that the knowledgeable will recognise the presence of the accepted good design concepts in your garden. For many years these rules have been accepted as the proper way to do things, but it is *your* garden. The all-important factors which you have to follow are the five essential elements set out on page 89 and the rules for avoiding design pitfalls on page 104.

Basic principles

Simplicity

Professional landscapers generally aim for simplicity in their designs, but despite their advice over-fussy gardens outnumber the restrained ones. Before deciding to fill your plot with all sorts of shapes and features it is worth while looking at the advantages of the simple approach.

First of all, the work in an over-complex garden can be enormous. Mowing is a skilful operation when weaving between a complex of flower beds, while edging and weeding can be never-ending tasks. Dead-heading cannot be neglected and early watering of all those annuals you have planted is an essential job in dry weather. Secondly, a jumble of unlinked features will make your garden look smaller, and it will not have the restful feel of a garden which has simpler lines.

The professionals are right — it is not a good idea to fill a large garden with a collection of borders, beds, pathways etc which do not hang together, but we should not take this concept too far. Many people with tiny plots choose an over-fussy design so that they have the opportunity to potter outdoors for hours.

Balance

A garden should be balanced. This does not mean that it should be strictly symmetrical with the right hand side being a mirror image of the left. In fact clear-cut symmetry is generally not a good idea in the home garden and there should be marked differences in design between the two halves. But it still has to be balanced, and the easiest way to do this is to imagine the left and right side of the garden on an enormous scales — if one side would clearly outweigh the other then the garden is not balanced. This is not quite as easy as it sounds — a dense leafy evergreen such as lawson's cypress is 'heavier' than a taller, more spreading open tree such as silver birch.

Unity

This word is used by garden designers to describe the way they make sure that the various parts of the garden blend into a harmonious whole. This does not mean that the result should be dull or unexciting. All sorts of variations and patterns are possible within an old-world garden or a modern formal one, but a piece of abstract sculpture would be quite out of place in a garden of old urns and old-fashioned roses as would be a wildflower area in an architectural garden.

A useful way of promoting unity is to make sure that the materials used for building walls belong to the same family as the walls of the house. They need not be identical in shape or colour, but weathered brick walls linked with an old brick house will give a feeling of unity. Avoiding the use of too many types of paving materials is also important — mixing artificial stone slabs, bricks, crazy paving, grass and gravel would certainly create a feeling of disharmony!

Contrast

It must seem odd to have both unity and contrast in a list of the basic principles of good design and actually on the same page! They are after all direct opposites. Unity means that there should be a feeling of harmony in the garden — contrast means that there should be a marked difference between things in the garden.

There is actually no problem — both have a role to play. As described above, you should aim to give the overall design a basic feeling of unity without having features which do not belong. Within that scheme of things there is a place for contrast, and that applies especially to the plants in the beds and borders. Don't just aim to have contrasting flower colours to provide eye-catching interest — yellow next to violet, orange close to blue etc. There should also be contrast in plant and leaf shape — feathery foliage next to large-leaved plants and upright shrubs next to bushy ones.

Scale

Scale is a designer term for ensuring that the height, width and length of the various living and non-living elements of the garden are in proportion. It is usual to think first of all of the dangers of having items which are just too big. Make sure that the mature plant height of any tree or shrub you buy will be in keeping with the garden — a basic piece of advice which continues to be given and continues to be ignored. The main problem is impulse buying — a weeping willow or japanese larch is bought at the garden centre because it 'looks so nice'. In a few years time there is the constant need to prune back as the giant tries to get to its natural height.

Less obvious but equally important is the necessity to avoid features which are too small. A tiny patio attached to a large and impressive house will look all wrong as will a small bed in a large expanse of lawn. Not too big and not too small, but this should never be taken to mean that a standard height is the thing to aim for. Even in a tiny plot a large-leaved architectural plant can provide a welcome focal point.

Interest

This is a very simple principle — there should be items in the garden which will make the observer go over to look at them. The item may be an especially attractive flower, or a plant that the visitor has never seen before, a piece of statuary or a koi pond. The interest point may be obvious as soon as you step out in the garden, but your skill as a designer is to ensure that at least some of these interest points are not immediately in view. In designer terms there should be 'mystery' as you approach the point of interest, 'tension' as you get close, and finally 'surprise' when you at last reach the hidden focal point. For us it is much simpler — just make sure that you have several focal points in the garden which catch the eye, and make sure that you cannot see them all when you stand on the patio or at the entrance to the back garden.

Shape and size

The introduction to this chapter stressed the point that it is *your* garden and within reason the only thing that matters is that the design should appeal to you. It is important, however, that you should take the size and shape of the plot into consideration as these really do limit what you can do to make it attractive.

It is only natural for a keen gardener to try to fill the area with as many plants and features as possible. Garden design bureaux look with amazement at some of the wants lists sent to them. The essentials are there, of course – lawn, garden shed, flower beds etc. Then there is all the rest – rose bed, fish pond, vegetable plot, rockery, play area, sundial and ..... If you have an acre or two then it may be no problem, but on a small plot it really is out of the question. Something must go from the list – some open area is vital in an average-sized standard garden if it is not to suffer from horticultural indigestion.

You also have to adapt your ideas to the shape of the garden. A long and narrow plot needs to be divided into several areas if it is not to look like a long passage-way. A square garden can be depressingly box-like. It will help if you have curved borders at the corners to break the line — circular beds or features also help.

Colour

There are all sorts of dos and don'ts on the use of colour in the garden — the best idea is to read the most important rules laid down by the experts and then use the ideas which fit in with your personal likes and dislikes.

Some of the basics of leaf and flower colour choice have been described on page 69. Put warm colours (reds, yellows etc) to the front and the cool ones (blues and greens) at the back to extend the length of the garden or make the border look wider. Aim for splashes of colour rather than a spotty mixture and use the same colour in various parts of the garden to give a feeling of unity.

There are three ways of putting colours together in an harmonious way — that is in a way in which they will 'go together'. The boldest approach is to create a contrasting scheme in which colours at opposite sides of the colour wheel are used — oranges with blues, yellows with violet, or reds with green. The effect is either dramatic or garish, depending on your point of view. The most restful way is to match analogous colours which lie next to each other on the colour wheel — blues with purples, or reds and yellows with orange flowers are examples. The most subtle use of colour is the monochromatic scheme where tints and shades of the same colour are used — the white or blue garden in the stately home is an example.

Whites and greys are used to bring out the best in other colours. They are used to add interest to pastel-coloured schemes or to remove the jarring effect of garish ones by dividing the bright colours.

Add height to the garden

The beauty of your garden will be enhanced if you have a mixture of heights. To some extent this can be achieved by having a range of plant sizes — column-like conifers, spreading shrubs, low-growing plants and carpeting ground covers. Remember that a tall feature reasonably close to the house will make the garden look longer. Planting climbers against the house wall is nearly always a good idea — the garden is extended upwards.

You will need more than a range of plant heights if you are to avoid the flat-earth policy which seems to affect so many plots. There should be some planted soil surfaces above the general ground level, and there are several ways of achieving this result. Planted tubs are an age-old method — as valuable as ever for providing colour and interest near the house. A rockery is another way of having living plants above ground level, but it must be properly constructed and maintained — see page 18. If you have a sloping site the obvious answer is to create one or more terraces with brick or stone retaining walls. Spreading rockery perennials can be planted at the front of these terraces to cascade downwards and soften the lines of the wall.

On a level site the answer is to build one or more raised beds. These will help to relieve the monotony of a flat garden, but there are other important advantages as outlined on page 70. Retaining walls can be built from a variety of materials — stone, reconstituted stone, brick, wood, split logs etc. Using dry stone walling gives the added advantage of allowing plants to be grown in the crevices of the retaining wall.

Hide eyesores

For eyesores which cannot be removed you will have to employ some form of screening. The usual answer is a decorative wall, a fence covered with russian vine, ivy or climbing roses, or a line of quick-growing conifers. These methods of screening are not the only ways of hiding eyesores. In fact, flat screening can have its problems — if it is large and eye-catching it can serve as a focal point which draws attention to the partly-hidden eyesore. It is sometimes better to have an irregular-shaped and three-dimensional feature such as a wide-spreading bush between the window and the undesirable view.

Create a permanent skeleton

The garden should contain a fixed year-round frame-work rather than looking like an over-sized windowbox. There should be a definite feeling of maturity, and this calls for the presence of permanent objects. Ornaments are useful — arches, sundials, fountains, walled areas and the rest, but you have to turn to shrubs and trees to provide the basic skeleton. Lack of space is no excuse — there are compact woody plants which can provide winter tracery when the annuals and the stems of border plants have disappeared.

Have evergreen and deciduous woody plants

Garden books abound with photographs of the scene in full summer, but the appearance in mid winter is largely ignored. In many gardens, however, we have to look at the garden for several months when all the leaves and flowers have gone. Evergreens seem to be the answer and of course some evergreens with grey, yellow, green or purple leaves are necessary, but the deciduous shrubs and trees have an equally important role to play. Most of the beautiful flowering types belong here, and there is also seasonal change.

Beware of the pitfalls

Don't be over-ambitious

Before you draw up the Design Plan you must face up to your limitations in time, money, ability, garden knowledge and health. There is no point in planning for a heated greenhouse unless you accept the annual cost of heating it in winter and the year-round work involved in watering, ventilating and so on.

Changing levels always involves more work than the gardener expects. You can't just cart the excess soil from a high spot to raise the height of another area. The topsoil must be first removed, the subsoil graded and the topsoil then replaced.

Laying paving slabs, bricklaying, concreting and cutting down large trees are not jobs to be undertaken lightly if you have never tackled them before. Get a professional to do the work if you can afford it. If that is not possible then read about the technique, speak to a knowledgeable friend and get him (or her) to help.

Few aspects of gardening give more pleasure than growing vegetables successfully ... and few take more time. If you have little time to spare do not incorporate a large vegetable patch in the design.

Don't commit the lawn sins

Just a patch of grass, perhaps, but a lot of thought should go into its design. The actual shape is up to you, but avoid tight or fussy curves and awkward corners. You should aim to have a surface free from bumps and hollows, but a gentle and even slope is acceptable. Grass will grow happily in sun or partial shade, but in deep shade it will never produce a satisfactory, tightly-knit turf.

The first sin is to extend the lawn into a completely sunless area. The second sin is to extend the lawn right up to a wall or path — a grass-free mowing strip should be maintained all round the lawn to make edging easier. The third sin is having a path which leads directly on to the lawn and stops at the edge. The regular traffic at this point will cause excessive wear and compaction. The fourth sin is to have narrow grass strips between beds and/or borders — the strips should be at least 75 cm to facilitate easy mowing.

The upkeep of grass banks is quite practical with the advent of the hover mower, but you should not extend the lawn over a bank with a slope of more than 30°. Finally, do not clutter up the lawn with objects which will make mowing difficult — examples include heavy seats, large flower pots and leafy trees.

Don't choose the wrong plants

When drawing up your planting plan check on the characteristics of each tree, shrub and herbaceous perennial before making your choice. Do this by looking in books, catalogues or on the internet. You will want to know the plant's expected height at maturity, flowering season and the colour of the blooms, but you must also find out the expected spread of a tree or shrub and its light and soil type requirements.

Nearly all bedding plants and rockery perennials thrive best in full sun, but numerous shrubs and border plants will flourish in partial shade. Make sure that your plant list matches the conditions under which the plants will have to grow. Failure to do this is asking for trouble — for example some plants will thrive in chalky soil but many would fail miserably. See pages 76 - 77 for further advice.

STEP 4

WRITE A REMOVALS LIST

You have decided on a style and you have a site plan of the garden. You will also have a rough idea of the sort of design you wish to create. If it is to be a standard garden then you will have thought whether you want it to be formal, informal or a mixture of both — a simple basic garden or an ornate de-luxe one.

Towards this end you should prepare a Removals List — things that are to go. This is usually a simple task if only a small amount of remodelling is planned — removing a garden shed, filling in a fussy flower bed on the lawn or getting rid of the sand-box now that the children have grown up. It is even easier when moving into a newly-built house — just get rid of the builders' rubbish!

Do think carefully before deciding to add a major item to your Removals List when remodelling an established garden. The removal of a large feature can leave a gaping bare patch which is much more extensive than you imagined it would be. Removing a path seems such a simple idea until you start trying to lift the stones. Old trees and ugly hedges are a special case. They may have reached the end of their useful life and then it is right to add them to your list, but in many cases renewal pruning as outlined on pages 39 - 46 can turn an eyesore into a vigorous and attractive plant in a couple of seasons.

A golden rule is to try to fit outstanding plants and/or features into your plan. Trees provide a living skeleton for and a feeling of maturity to your garden, but there are times when some trees have to go, and here it is necessary to check that they are not subject to a Tree Preservation Order.

16 Bradbury Ave
Cheltenham

REMOVALS LIST

The narrow annual flower border around the house has to go — it is so dull all winter long.

The mixed border has to be changed. The present one is too long and too boring, but I do want a border and I want to keep as many of the plants as possible.

The round flower bed at the bottom of the lawn. It is such a formal feature at a spot where the garden should have a more informal look.

The vegetable plot has to be changed. I want to grow some vegetables but the present site is so much trouble.

The tall sycamore in front of the vegetable garden has to go — it is not attractive and casts too much shade.

STEP 5

START THE DESIGN PLAN

You have prepared a Site Plan and made a note of the garden style you have chosen. Towards this goal you have listed the features you have decided to remove, and in Step 3 you have got to know something about the principles of good design.

It is now time to start work on the Design Plan. Make a tracing of the scale plan prepared in Step 2, leaving out the red, yellow and blue shaded areas. In addition omit the items on your Removals List. This will include both features which will not appear in the new design and also those which are to have a different shape. Include only the items which will remain unaltered. This new plan will eventually become your Design Plan. Take a photocopy and enlarge it to fill nearly all of the sheet of paper. Take a number of copies so you can develop your ideas — you will certainly have second thoughts after your first attempt!

If there are to be major changes or if you are starting from scratch there is much to do before you are ready to finalise the plan. It is necessary to draw up a Wants List — for each new feature you will have studied the advantages, limitations, price etc of the various items. You can use one or more of the photocopies to rough out a general idea of the form of your new garden, but it is too early to prepare a final Design Plan at this stage.

It may be that you are planning only a minor alteration and have a clear idea of just what you want. In that case you can draw the features on the plan and if the time is right you are ready to start work — move to Step 9.

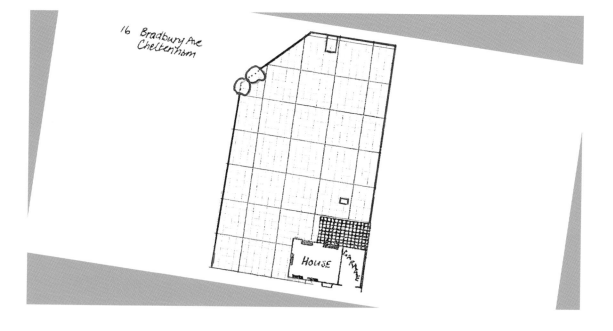

STEP 6

WRITE A WANTS LIST

It is now time to draw up a Wants List so that you can get on with the Design Plan. Before beginning study the preliminary plan you have prepared to see what space you will have available once the items earmarked for removal have gone. Look at the site too, of course — some people find it useful to take photographs at this stage so that they have a picture of the garden when drawing up the Wants List and working on the Design Plan.

So off you go to prepare a list of the things you want to include. There will be basic garden features — rose bed, pond, paved sitting-out area or other desirable item which is missing. Add trees and shrubs you have seen and would like to include — weeping cherry, pampas grass etc. Finally, the non-living features — some attractive like a greenhouse, summer house or patio, and others mundane, such as a rotary washing line or a compost bin. It is not just a matter of deciding on the type of feature you would like in your garden — a greenhouse, sundial etc. As noted on page 106 you will have to decide on which ones you plan to buy. Read pages 108 - 117, look in the catalogues and magazines, watch the TV programmes and collect leaflets. Best of all, look at other people's gardens.

There are two general rules concerning the Wants List. Don't try to pack too much into your garden. It would be surprising if this list didn't need pruning once the first draft was completed. A garden should not look like a garden centre — there should be large plain areas to dramatise the busy and colourful spots. The second rule is that you should plan for the future. Include a play area even though the baby is still at the crawling stage. Include a much-wanted greenhouse even though funds will not be available for a couple of years. Simply add these as 'items to follow' to remind you to leave space on the Design Plan.

16 Bradbury Ave
Cheltenham

WANTS LIST

A decent sized lawn, free from hard-to-cut bits. Paths at the side but not through the middle.

A mixed border along the west fence with a more interesting slope than the present one.

A new vegetable garden.

The patio is fine, but it does need some pots, wall plants etc.

The overall design I should like is a standard garden with a formal area with beds close to the house and an informal feel towards the back.

Some more trees, especially near the back. It would be nice to have some conifers and other evergreens to give winter colour.

A pergola or arch on which I can grow a clematis or honeysuckle.

A hidden-away place for the compost heap.

Some nice paved paths.

FEATURES

Paths & Drives

A path is designed for two-footed and two-wheeled traffic — a drive carries four-wheeled traffic. Nowadays there is a host of different paving materials and this makes selection difficult. For out-of-the-way walkways such as in the vegetable garden you can use purely functional materials such as compacted earth, concrete and bark chippings, but in nearly all cases the paths and drives have a decorative as well as a utilitarian purpose. The drive is the first part of the garden the visitor may see, and paths often form a clearly visible skeleton to the garden. So choose with care — see below. Combining different materials can reduce the danger of dullness (see illustration) but take care not to mix too many paving materials.

A few rules. Make the path wide enough — 60 cm is the minimum for the average garden but 1 m is better. It should slope (minimum 1 in 100) to prevent water standing after rain. If constructed next to the house, the surface must be at least 15 cm below the damp-proof course. Finally, seek planning permission if you propose to create a drive which will make a new access on to the road.

BRICKS or BLOCKS		No heavy lifting is necessary. Bricks make an excellent path where an old-world look is required. Don't use ordinary bricks — ask for paving ones. As an alternative you can use brick-like blocks (paviors) made of clay or concrete
STONE or SLABS		Natural stone gives an air of luxury, but slate, sandstone, yorkstone etc are very expensive. Slabs made of concrete or reconstituted stone are a much more popular and inexpensive alternative these days
MACADAM		This mixture of stone chippings with tar or bitumen is the favourite material for drives and has several names — asphalt, black top, 'Tarmac' etc. This is not a job for an amateur — choose your contractor with care
CRAZY PAVING		Laying flagstones or paving slabs can be heavy work and you generally have to keep to straight lines — with crazy paving the pieces are smaller and the informal effect means that you don't have to aim for a perfect fit
CONCRETE		Concrete is criticised by many for its austere look, but it remains a popular material for both paths and drives. It is durable, fairly inexpensive and suitable for curving or irregular pathways. Laying concrete is for the fit, strong and knowledgeable
WOOD or BARK		Pulverised or shredded bark is a popular material for paths in woodland — it is soft underfoot but requires topping up every few years. Sawn log rounds are sometimes set in the shredded bark. Decking (see page 112) is sometimes used
GRAVEL or PEBBLES		Gravel is by far the cheapest material. Shingle (small stones smoothed by water) and true gravel (stone chips from a quarry) are the types available. Large rounded pebbles are sometimes used for small decorative areas
PATTERN-PRINTED CONCRETE		A post-war development for paths, drives and patios. A concrete-based mix is poured over the area and a roller is taken over the surface before it has set. The roller leaves an embossed pattern in the form of blocks, slabs or crazy paving

Patio

A patio is a hard-surfaced area which is usually but not always attached to the house and is used for relaxation, enjoyment and perhaps entertaining. There may be just a small area of paving slabs with a plastic table and a couple of chairs, or it may be a multi-tiered structure with beds, pond, pergolas and permanent features.

The size should generally be in keeping with the size of the garden. Aim for at least 4 sq.m for each person who will eat or lounge on it — modify the dimensions slightly so that the need to cut slabs, blocks etc is kept to a minimum. The usual shape is a rectangle — an irregular shape may be more interesting but slab-cutting to fit curves is a laborious job.

The best place is adjoining the back of the house, especially if there are patio doors — the task of taking out food and drink and bringing in cushions is greatly simplified. It is not the only place — afternoon sun and protection from the prevailing wind are even more important than saving labour.

For suitable paving materials, see page 112. A single paving material should dominate the patio, and this should be in keeping with nearby paths and walls. Some designers like to introduce a second paving material, but do resist a patchwork quilt effect.

Mark out the proposed area with canes and string before work begins. Sit in the space, walk about, bring in chairs and tables. Is it really the right size? Remember that if you don't have the necessary skill, strength or time it will be necessary to bring in a landscaping company — as stressed on page 125 you should obtain quotes before work starts. Enrol a willing helper if it is to be a DIY job.

Basic patio

Designer patio

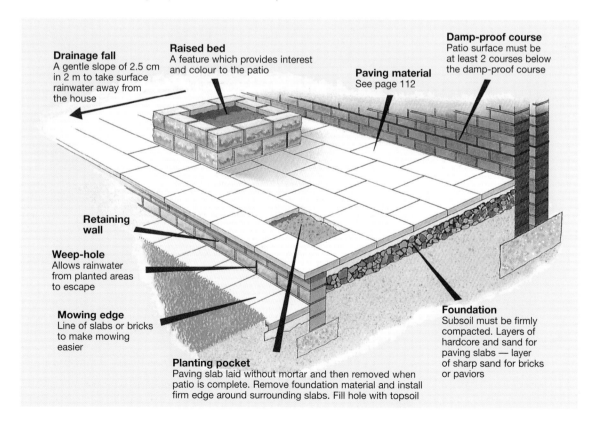

Drainage fall
A gentle slope of 2.5 cm in 2 m to take surface rainwater away from the house

Raised bed
A feature which provides interest and colour to the patio

Paving material
See page 112

Damp-proof course
Patio surface must be at least 2 courses below the damp-proof course

Retaining wall

Weep-hole
Allows rainwater from planted areas to escape

Mowing edge
Line of slabs or bricks to make mowing easier

Planting pocket
Paving slab laid without mortar and then removed when patio is complete. Remove foundation material and install firm edge around surrounding slabs. Fill hole with topsoil

Foundation
Subsoil must be firmly compacted. Layers of hardcore and sand for paving slabs — layer of sharp sand for bricks or paviors

Arches & Pergolas

An arch is a relatively narrow walk-through structure — a pergola is an extended archway or a series of linked arches. There are three basic rules. The first one is that an arch or pergola should have a definite purpose — do not use it as an isolated feature in the lawn at the side of a flower bed. The classical use is to cover part or all of a pathway with plant-bedecked vertical and overhead supports. Next, make sure that material and design fit in with the house and garden style — rustic poles look attractive in a traditional setting but would look out of place in ultra-modern surroundings. The third vital rule is that the structure must be strong enough and sufficiently well-anchored to withstand gale-force winds.

You can make a wooden arch from scratch using rustic poles or sawn timber, but it is much more usual these days to buy a kit or ready-made one. Use preservative-treated wood and rust-proof nails and screws. Wood, of course, is not the only material — a wide range of plastic-coated and all-metal arches are available. Make sure it is large enough — the height should be at least 2 m and the width 1.25 m or more.

The pergola was once a feature of the country estate, but now you will find them everywhere. There are two reasons for this increase in popularity — there is a wide variety of prefabricated kits nowadays and the patio boom has created a widespread need for a semi-enclosed spot which links house and garden. Some people prefer the oriental pergola to the traditional one — here the cross beams have bevelled rather than square-cut edges.

A typical arch — apex-topped, trellis-sided and flanked by a simple picket fence. Make sure that the posts are set firmly in the ground

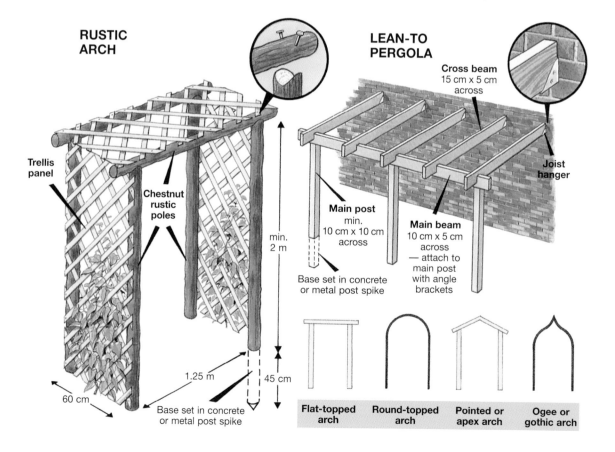

RUSTIC ARCH

Trellis panel

Chestnut rustic poles

min. 2 m

1.25 m

60 cm

45 cm

Base set in concrete or metal post spike

LEAN-TO PERGOLA

Cross beam
15 cm x 5 cm
across

Joist hanger

Main post
min.
10 cm x 10 cm
across

Base set in concrete
or metal post spike

Main beam
10 cm x 5 cm
across
— attach to
main post
with angle
brackets

| Flat-topped arch | Round-topped arch | Pointed or apex arch | Ogee or gothic arch |

Play area

Any parent with small children will know the benefits of having one or more child-friendly features in the garden. The range is shown below — just a couple can mean getting them outdoors and out from under your feet, and for them a chance to play in the fresh air.

It all sounds such a good idea, but there can be a few problems. The first one is boredom — pushing a child outdoors with just a ball can mean exclusion from all their toys indoors. Expensive equipment and solid playhouses are not the only answer — simple objects for their make-believe games are often preferred. A second minor problem is garden damage — pots are knocked over, stems are broken, etc. You can reduce the risk of damage by giving them a small piece of the garden for themselves. Examples are a sand box, swing or fenced-off area.

The big problem is safety, and when redesigning your garden remember that over 100,000 children are treated in hospital every year as a result of garden accidents. The danger age is between 2 and 5 when they are active but with little sense of danger.

Go through the following check-list. Play areas for small children should be in sight of the kitchen window and close enough to hear their calls. Put some form of soft matting under a swing, slide or climbing frame. Make sure that small children can't wander into the road. Put tools, machinery and chemicals away. Keep play areas well away from the greenhouse and keep paths free from moss and algae. Buy good quality play equipment and don't make your own if you are unskilled. If you do, then sink nails and screws below the surface. A toddler can drown in 10 cm of water — never allow a child to go near a pond or paddling pool without supervision.

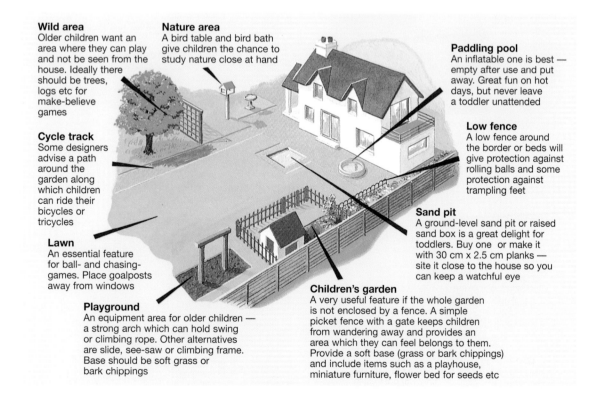

Wild area
Older children want an area where they can play and not be seen from the house. Ideally there should be trees, logs etc for make-believe games

Nature area
A bird table and bird bath give children the chance to study nature close at hand

Paddling pool
An inflatable one is best — empty after use and put away. Great fun on hot days, but never leave a toddler unattended

Cycle track
Some designers advise a path around the garden along which children can ride their bicycles or tricycles

Low fence
A low fence around the border or beds will give protection against rolling balls and some protection against trampling feet

Lawn
An essential feature for ball- and chasing-games. Place goalposts away from windows

Sand pit
A ground-level sand pit or raised sand box is a great delight for toddlers. Buy one or make it with 30 cm x 2.5 cm planks — site it close to the house so you can keep a watchful eye

Playground
An equipment area for older children — a strong arch which can hold swing or climbing rope. Other alternatives are slide, see-saw or climbing frame. Base should be soft grass or bark chippings

Children's garden
A very useful feature if the whole garden is not enclosed by a fence. A simple picket fence with a gate keeps children from wandering away and provides an area which they can feel belongs to them. Provide a soft base (grass or bark chippings) and include items such as a playhouse, miniature furniture, flower bed for seeds etc

Paved areas

The dividing line between paths and paved areas is a narrow one. The essential difference is that paths are designed for foot or light vehicle traffic and so have a practical purpose — a paved area is basically to support sitting or standing people and so the decorative element is more important.

Not surprisingly most of the materials used for the construction of paths and drives (see page 108) can be used for paving, but there are two restrictions if the area is to be used as a patio. Loose material such as gravel or bark should be avoided for overall surfacing and so should items like cobblestones and granite setts which feel uncomfortable underfoot.

A single material should be used for paving a patio, and this should be in keeping with nearby paths and walls. The introduction of a second paving material can sometimes be attractive — popular examples are a line of paviors around large expanses of paving slabs or a patch of cobblestones set within a stone or paving slab patio.

PAVING SLABS

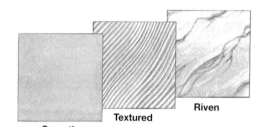

Riven

Textured

Smooth

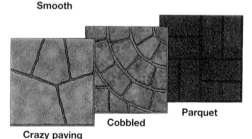

Parquet

Cobbled

Crazy paving

Colour and arrangement are a matter of taste, but most designers advise against multicoloured and chessboard schemes. A mixture of square and rectangular slabs tends to give a more interesting surface than one made up entirely of squares, and unnatural colours are best avoided. The cheapest slabs are 4 cm thick concrete ones, but it really is worth investing in reconstituted stone slabs.

DECKING

Wooden paving blends in well with surrounding trees and shrubs, and its popularity continues to grow. Use western red cedar — an alternative is an ordinary softwood which has been pressure-impregnated with a preservative. For DIY decking fix planks to stout wooden joists which are stood on brick supports — a 10 mm gap is left between the planks. It is much easier to lay 60 cm x 1 m timber tiles which are laid on sand over gravel.

BRICKS & PAVIORS

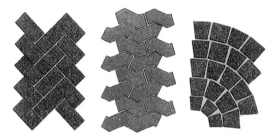

Bricks (Special Quality grade) are a good choice in old-world and informal settings — their great advantage is the way they can be used for irregular or curved areas without the need for cutting. Concrete and clay-based paviors (blocks) have similar advantages and are available in several colours and shapes.

CRAZY PAVING

A favourite surface until concrete and reconstituted stone slabs came along. It is worth considering if you want an informal look — yorkstone is the popular type but there are others. Broken concrete slabs are an inexpensive alternative — some paving suppliers have them available at a very low price.

STONE

Natural stone is expensive, difficult to lay and not too easy to find. It is, however, still the only paving choice for many traditionalists and you may feel that the special and unique charm of yorkstone outweighs the disadvantages.

TILES

Square tiles which are about 2.5 cm thick are an easy-to-handle paving material for patios. Concrete ones are available in several sizes and colours — some too bright for the average garden. For the architectural or mediterranean-style garden there are colourful ceramic tiles.

Pond

A garden pond provides so much interest for most of the year, but only if the pond is constructed and stocked in the right way. All too often we see murky green water which is overrun by weeds. The cause is generally a combination of doing the wrong things at the start and then failing to do the few necessary things once the pond has become established. Consult pages 52 - 54 if you have a problem. Read the paragraphs below if you plan to have a pond.

Small formal pond

SIZE
You will need a surface area of at least 4 sq.m if the water is to stay clear — the depth will have to be 60 cm or more if you plan to have several types of fish.

SITE
Choose a sunny spot away from trees — dead leaves decompose to produce salts and gases which are harmful to fish and encourage green algae.

STYLE
There are two basic styles. The formal pond outline is clearly defined and the shape is either geometrical (square, oblong etc) or gently curved. It is separated from other garden features and is often used as a centrepiece. The informal pond outline is not clearly defined — it merges into an adjoining feature or features. The shape is irregular.

Large informal pond

CONSTRUCTION MATERIALS
There are three basic materials. Concrete was once the basic material but its time has now passed. The rigid or moulded pool makes pond-making a much easier task. Vacuum-formed plastic ones are fairly short-lived and are only semi-rigid — it is better to choose a fibreglass one. To make a larger pond and/or one of your own design you must use a flexible liner. Polyethylene sheeting was the original material but it is no longer a good choice. PVC is a better choice, but for life-long reliability you should choose butyl — a synthetic rubber sheeting.

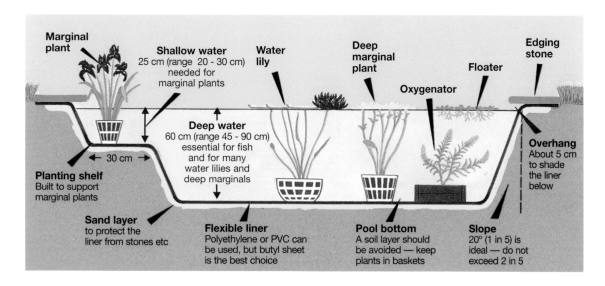

Greenhouse

Here you can raise plants, keep half-hardy perennials over winter and grow tomatoes. In addition it is a cosy retreat from workaday worries and the weather. Unfortunately greenhouse growing is perhaps the most labour-intensive of all aspects of gardening — consider having as much automatic equipment as you can afford.

SIZE

The minimum satisfactory size is 2.5 m x 2 m — it is much more difficult to control the temperature and avoid draughts in a small house than in a large one. The ventilation area in the roof should be at least 20% of the floor space.

SITE

Choose a sunny site, away from buildings which could shade out winter sun. Avoid erecting a greenhouse close to trees — 10 m is the recommended distance.

CONSTRUCTION MATERIALS

Wood is the most attractive material, but cheap softwood may rot after a few years if it has not been pressure-treated. Choose rot-proof wood such as teak or western red cedar, but it is expensive and so aluminium has taken over as the most popular material. It loses slightly more heat than wood at night and aluminium houses are more difficult to erect than wooden ones, but these drawbacks are minor. On the credit side it needs no maintenance, more light is admitted, re-glazing is a simple matter and warping does not occur. uPVC requires nothing more than an occasional washing down.

HEATING

A cold house is unheated. It is used for tomatoes and cucumbers in summer, chrysanthemums in autumn, and alpines and bulbs in winter. In a cool house you can grow greenhouse plants such as Azalea, Cineraria etc and half-hardy bedding plants for the garden. You will need some form of heating — electricity is generally considered the best choice. It is clean, easily controlled and disease-promoting humidity is not produced. With a warm house you can grow semi-tropical plants, but costs are high.

COLD GREENHOUSE
Unheated except by the sun

**minimum temperature -2° C
when outside temperature falls to -7° C**

COOL GREENHOUSE
Heater required during the cooler months

minimum temperature 7° C

WARM GREENHOUSE
Heater required during most months

minimum temperature 13° C

Span roof
The traditional style has vertical sides. Efficient use of space and heat. Winter heat loss is reduced if lower part is enclosed. Choose an all-glass version for growing-bag and border crops

Lean-to
Useful for a south- or west-facing wall. The house wall stores heat so the fuel bill is reduced. This is the usual conservatory pattern — an interconnecting door makes it part of the home

Dutch light
Sloping sides and an even span roof — the angled glass makes it warmer and brighter than a traditional span roof house. Also more stable, but supporting upright plants from floor to roof is more difficult

Three-quarter span
More airy and more comfortable to work in than a lean-to — useful for growing wall plants such as grapes and figs. Expensive, so it is usual to choose between a span roof house or a lean-to

Containers

As shown below there are places all round the garden for containers. Wherever you need a compact splash of colour or a green focal point there is a type of container to fill the bill. The increased use of containers is not difficult to understand. The dramatic growth in the number of patios has meant that there are now more bare paved areas to clothe in millions of gardens, and people are now more aware than ever of the benefits of container gardening. Ground is not needed and plants can be put right next to the house. Plants not suited to your soil can be grown, tender plants can be put outside in summer and there is less chance of pest damage. Finally, plants can be moved away once the flowering season is over.

Many advantages, but there is one important disadvantage. Frequent watering is essential in summer and this may mean using a watering can or hose daily during a dry spell. Containers with vertical sides will need less frequent watering than those with sharply sloping sides. In addition feeding is required at regular intervals.

Containers are usually bought as such from garden centres, hardware sheds or mail order companies, but there are kits for wooden containers and a wide range of non-garden items can be used — kitchen sinks, chimney pots etc. In a tiny garden the container display may be more extensive than the open ground features, but in most cases the troughs and pots are restricted to just a few well-defined areas. When grouping containers it is generally wise to have a single or a limited range of types (wood, plastic etc) but a decent range of sizes.

Making the right choice is not easy. Obviously you will be influenced by your personal taste and the depth of your pocket, but there are some general guidelines. Make sure it is large enough. Large containers do not have to be watered as frequently as small ones. On an exposed site you will need a tub which is at least 45 cm across and 30 cm high if tall plants are to be grown. Make sure that size and material are in keeping with the house and garden — an ornate pot may be out of place in a modern garden. Finally, check that there is at least one drainage hole (2 cm or more across) every 10 - 15 cm.

The same plant in the same pot. A line of evenly-spaced terracotta pots planted with hydrangeas provides a feeling of unity

The muted colour of the unstained Versailles tub gives an extra brilliance to this spring display of wallflowers and pansies

Front door & Porch
An excellent place for containers — either singly or as a pair of matched pots. Careful selection and maintenance are essential as the display must always be in first-class condition

Path or Steps liner
A line of identical pots or troughs can enhance the appearance of a plain walkway or flight of steps

Focal point
A large container or a group of smaller containers can be used to provide a focal point. Attractive trees and shrubs have an important role to play here — pots and plants must be in scale with the surroundings

Patio
The favourite place these days for free-standing containers. The starkness of bare walls and paving slabs is relieved by the presence of plants. Bedding plants and bulbs are the usual planting material

Balcony
Trailing plants to grow over the container and climbers to clothe the railings are widely grown. Use a lightweight container and a peat-based compost. Exposure to strong winds can be a problem

Hanging basket
A popular feature these days — about a third of gardens have one. The best site is partly sunny during the day and is protected from strong winds. Remember daily watering may be necessary in summer

Window sill
Window boxes add colour and interest to dull walls and windows. The construction material and its colour should not detract from the plants — make sure that the box is firmly attached

Greenhouse
Planting vegetables in the border soil can create all sorts of problems — the greenhouse is usually filled with pots and growing bags which contain suitable growing media

Walls

The basic difference between a wall and a fence is that there is a firm foundation along the entire length of a wall. Boundary walls are chosen rather than fencing when maximum privacy, permanence and noise reduction are required. A high wall may seem a good idea, but there are problems — cost, bye-law restrictions, creation of turbulence in windy weather etc. Internal walls are an important feature in many gardens. There are screen walls to enclose areas or hide unsightly views and there are retaining walls as shown below.

BRICKS

Clay bricks are available in all sorts of colours and textures — choose Special Quality ones for exposed situations, wall tops etc. Concrete bricks are much less popular — they are lighter to lift than blocks but are more difficult to lay.

BLOCKS

Blocks made from natural stone, concrete and reconstituted stone are much larger than a brick. Laying time is reduced, and blocks with a 'natural' face mask minor imperfections. As with bricks a sound foundation is vital.

Stone blocks Constructing a wall of limestone, granite or sandstone is not a practical idea.

Decorative concrete blocks These blocks have a moulded face and can be used to build a head-high wall without piers. Cheaper than reconstituted stone blocks, but they look less natural. The standard thickness is 10 cm — a popular length is 45 cm.

Screen blocks Square concrete blocks are available which are pierced with a variety of patterns, and are made in numerous colours. They are stack bonded with each vertical mortar joint lining up with the one above and the one below.

Reconstituted stone blocks These blocks are the favourite garden walling material. Surface textures range from the near-smooth to the deeply-hewn pitched face. Low walls can be built on firm paving as well as on concrete footings. For dry (mortar-free) walling there are 15 cm wide blocks.

Most walls are now built with reconstituted stone blocks rather than bricks. An advantage is that units of various sizes can be used

Screen walls can provide an attractive feature. Here the screen is incorporated in a solid block wall

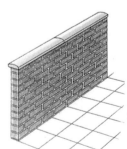

Free-standing wall

Basic example is the boundary wall. Maximum height of a brick wall without piers is 45 cm (10 cm thick wall) or 135 cm (21 cm thick wall). Higher walls need piers at 1 - 1½ m intervals

Light-duty retaining wall

The wall around a modest raised bed. The blocks are vertical and not sloping backwards. The wall should be just one block thick. Leave weep-holes at the base and paint inside with bituminous paint

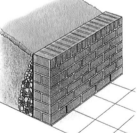

Heavy-duty retaining wall

This wall has to withstand a great deal of pressure — it should be at least 21 cm thick. Make sure it slopes slightly backwards and has weep-holes near the base. Line inside with plastic sheeting

Load-bearing wall

Not a common garden feature — but is required if you plan to erect a carport or brick conservatory. The simple rule is that you should leave this work to a professional if you do not have the necessary skill

Fences

A fence provides the quickest and usually the easiest way to mark the boundary of your property — if privacy is important a solid fence is the answer. Fences are more than boundary markers — they can be used to hide unsightly objects, separate sections of the garden, provide protection against the wind, act as supports for climbing plants and provide a way to keep children in (or out).

The range of materials for and the styles of fencing are much greater than for walling. Shown below are some of the more popular styles, but there are many others — closeboard fencing, wattle panels, chain link fencing, post and chain fencing etc. The basic choice of construction material is wood or concrete for the posts and wood or metal for the fence itself — for low-level fencing there are plastic fences. The fencing you pick should be in keeping with the style of both house and garden. Chestnut paling around a modern house is as much out of place as a chain-link fence around a cottage garden.

Where possible inspect both posts and panels before buying and check the following points. Posts should be made of hardwood or pressure-impregnated softwood. The pales should be neither bowed nor warped and all nails and staples should be rust-proof. There should be very few knots, and they should not measure more than 3 cm across. Post caps and panel capping rails are necessary.

One final point. Seek planning permission from your local authority before building a boundary wall or fence which is more than 2 m high — or 1 m high if it is to be erected adjacent to the road.

Ordinary trellis fencing without plants can look rather plain. Decorative types such as these wave-shaped panels are available

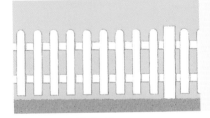

Interwoven panel
The most popular of the solid panel fences, made from thin strips of wood woven between a number of vertical stiffeners. Make sure that the wood strips fit closely together and are attached to the stiffeners

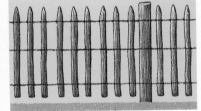

Chestnut paling
Bought as a roll and is attached to 2 or 3 strong wires stretched between posts at 2 m intervals. Not a thing of beauty but it is cheap, easy to erect and an effective barrier. Camouflage with shrubs and climbers

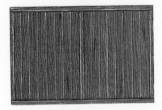

Lap panel
An alternative to the ever-popular interwoven panel — more expensive but more durable. The pales may be horizontal or vertical. Make sure that the overlap is adequate (about 2 cm)

Picket fence
The stout pales are rarely more than 1 m high and are attached to horizontal rails. Leave about 8 - 10 cm between the pales. The bottom of these pales should be 5 - 8 cm above the ground to prevent rotting

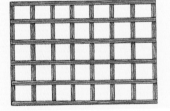

Trellis
Trellis made from thin strips of wood (laths) or larch poles (rustic work) arranged in a square or diamond pattern. It requires a stout holding frame and is rarely used as a boundary fence

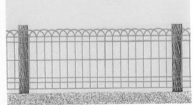

Wire picket fence
Nearly all the fences shown here are stout structures — wire picket fencing is at the other end of the scale. A series of small loops of plastic-coated wire are linked together to form a low fence for beds

STEP 7

COMPLETE THE DESIGN PLAN

We have at last reached the stage where a detailed plan has to be prepared, using the notes and drawings collected during Steps 1 - 6. As advised on page 107 it is a good idea to have collected photographs of gardens and features which appeal — these can be taken by you or cut from magazines.

It is now decision time — who is going to prepare this plan? For nearly everyone it is a simple choice — you will be your own designer. If so, go on to page 120 and carry on from there. As an aid you can try one of the many Garden Designer CD-ROMs which are available. Fun to use if you are a computer fan and many are very informative, but they do not give you the flexibility and freedom of a pencil and piece of graph paper. You can copy an example from a book of garden plans, but none of them will fit your site and aspect exactly.

You may feel that you do not have the necessary experience and/or expertise to create your own plan, in which case you will need professional help. The less expensive route is to use a Garden Planning Service — several magazines and organisations run such a service. There will not be a site visit, so send the lists and plans you have prepared so far. A better alternative is to employ a garden designer who will come to your garden. Here it is not necessary to have prepared a Site Plan or to have started the Design Plan, but it is a useful exercise in order to give a detailed summary of what you have and what you want, and to enable you and the designer to speak the same language. Under no circumstances should you merely hand over a few vague thoughts on a scrap of paper.

16 Bradbury Ave
Cheltenham

DESIGN PLAN

The garden design at 16 Bradbury Avenue was developed to give a clean and simple feel with the minimum of reorganisation of the garden spaces. This latter point is important as the clients will be doing the work in their spare time. Two lawns are included – a play lawn to the side and the main lawn to the rear. Both are bounded by mowing strips for ease of maintenance. A previously damp low area has been utilised to create a formal pool and a brick path sweeps around the western lawn edge. A new patio has been included at the sunny end of the garden and a pergola cuts through the mixed border to a secluded seating area. The vegetable plot now has formal paths and smaller, easy-to-manage beds. A bird table to disguise the manhole cover and two raised beds complete the scheme.

paul dracott garden designs

THE DESIGNER APPROACH

To find a designer you can ask a garden centre or look in your local telephone directory, but it is better to choose someone who has been recommended to you. Do look through the portfolio of work which has been done for other people and ask for a quote before work begins. The design below was prepared by Paul Dracott who was given the plans and lists from Steps 1 - 6. The reasons why he chose this design are given on the previous page.

DESIGN PLAN

1 Children's play lawn
2 Entrance paving
3 Raised flower beds
4 Formal pond
5 Main lawn
6 Brick path
7 Pergola
8 Secluded seating area
9 Bench
10 Existing Magnolia stellatas
11 Existing shed
12 Vegetable beds and paths
13 Paved utility area
14 Second patio
15 Brick mowing edge
16 Bird table
17 Existing main patio

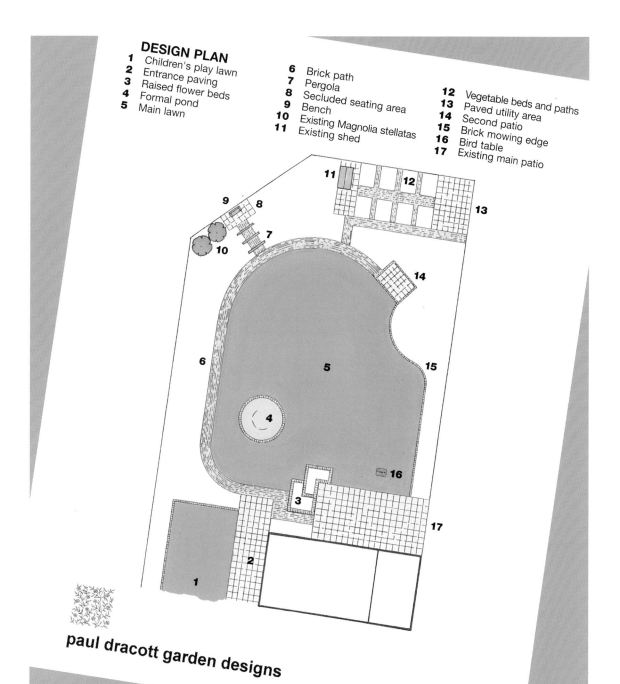

paul dracott garden designs

THE DIY APPROACH

Doing it yourself is, of course, the cheapest planning route but that is not the only advantage. You can spend much more time on the task than a professional, and you know better than anyone else what you like. Finally, there is the feeling of pride in having created a new garden from scratch.

1: Begin with a rough plan

Look at the questionnaire you filled in on page 90 and the Wants List you prepared at Step 6 (page 107). Now write down a 'must have' list and a 'like to have' one. In the example we have been working on the must-haves would include the large lawn, the altered mixed border, a vegetable plot, patio etc. Since preparing the original Wants List there may be other features you have decided to add — a pergola perhaps, or a swing for the children. A word of warning — do not make this list too large. The 'like to have' list can be longer — a pond in the wet area on the lawn perhaps, a rockery at the far end of the garden or maybe an extra sitting-out area.

Use one of the photocopies prepared at Step 5 (page 106) to start your rough plan. You will have decided on the style of garden and also whether it is to be formal or informal (page 93). Moving from a formal approach to a more informal feel at the back of the garden is an accepted good design technique, but to mix formal and informal features in the same area is rarely a good idea. At this stage you should map out the must-have features — the lawn, border, vegetable plot etc. Do not add any detail at this stage and do not try to fix definite dimensions. Just allocate space for all the major features and the like-to-haves you wish to include, walk around the garden with the plan to make sure you are happy and then get on with the finished plan. Don't rush this stage. You will no doubt change your mind several times and have to prepare several versions until you are ready to get on to that finished drawing.

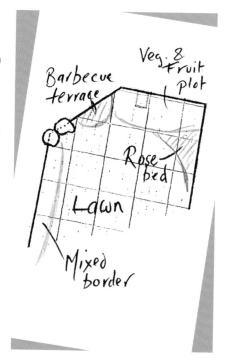

2: Draw the finished plan

It is now time to make a scale drawing using one of the photocopies from Step 5 (page 106) and the rough plan you have just prepared. In making your plans you should have kept both construction cost and maintenance time in mind. A koi pond may be highly desirable, but the cost may be prohibitive. A warm, large greenhouse would be a joy in winter, but the year-round work involved can make it a burden.

With the features which are to be included there are two important considerations before deciding on size and exact position. The first point to think about is that it is much cheaper to enlarge or reduce the size of some features (beds, borders, lawns etc) than to move them from one place to another. The second point to consider is aspect. Ponds, rockeries, greenhouses and beds for annuals need sunny sites away from trees. Turf grasses fail in deep shade — patios should be in sunshine for at least part of the day. Play areas and herb gardens are best sited close to the house. Whether you hide away the vegetable plot or leave it prominently exposed as your pride and joy is up to you.

Everything now has a place and a size, and the features can be drawn on the plan. You have remembered to avoid blocking attractive views and have made provision to hide eyesores either at this stage or in the Planting Scheme (page 122). Check that the family is happy. You have reached the stage when there is nothing more you can do, so take several photocopies and start work on the Planting Scheme.

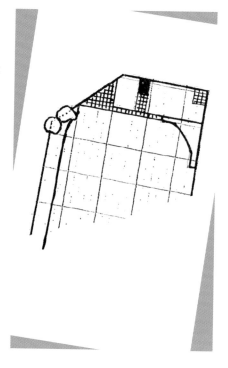

Awkward shapes

Long and narrow

Long and narrow plots are not uncommon and so many people have a garden which poses a problem. A long unbroken lawn bounded by straight borders along the sides will give the property an unappealing tube-like look, with the eye being drawn immediately to the far distance. The photograph shows the standard way to provide interest — turn the plot into a series of rooms. These can be separated by hedges or low fences, or you can have an open plan as illustrated

L-shaped

The usual answer is to continue the garden design around the corner as in the example shown here, and leave the owner to feel disappointed that the display has been shortened. It is generally a better idea to create a quite different arrangement in all or part of the leg around the corner so as to provide a surprise item — see page 102

Small and square

Low planting in a small and square garden which is surrounded by a close-board wooden fence can have a depressing box-like appearance. One of the answers is to have shrubs which hide the fence and have curved or irregular planting areas in the corners to hide the geometrical lines. Theoretically this dense planting should make the garden look smaller, but if there are tall trees and shrubs in the surrounding gardens the overall effect may be to enhance the size of the plot

STEP 8

ADD THE PLANTING SCHEME

You have produced a detailed outline of the non-living structures in the garden. The Design Plan shows the position of the lawn, but there are beds, borders, boundaries and perhaps other areas for which it is necessary to prepare a Planting Scheme. This will show how you propose to clothe the garden with the elements which will give it colour, variety, seasonal interest and life — the plants.

As with the preparation of the Design Plan it is once again decision time — who is going to prepare this scheme? The answer is the same — for nearly everyone it is the garden owner who puts the Planting Scheme together. This is a worrying prospect for many people but help is on hand if you lack experience. You can copy or adapt the planting schemes in gardening books — collections plus the necessary plans are offered in magazines. Be guided by others if you must but the basic rule remains that you should check the requirements of each plant in a reliable garden book and make sure that it will be happy in the conditions to be provided. If you propose to do your own thing and not use someone else's plan then it is vital to gather information. Cuttings from magazines, watching TV programmes and CD-ROMs are fine, but nothing can match looking around gardens to see what plants you like.

If you have used a designer for the Design Plan then he or she will be responsible for the Planting Scheme. If you are just creating a new border in an existing garden you can use a Garden Planning Service run by a magazine or horticultural organisation if you feel the job is beyond you.

16 Bradbury Ave
Cheltenham

PLANTING SCHEME

To achieve a balanced design the amount of planting has been increased. The main mixed border has been refurbished and extended towards the house with a border of spring bulbs and summer flowering perennials. The mixed border has been backed by climbers and a hedge of Lawson's cypress planted to screen an ugly view. At the foot of the garden a deep tree and shrub border has been added to give the garden depth and to separate the second patio from the vegetable garden. This flows into an herbaceous border designed to give a long season of interest, combining flowers with varied shapes. Close to the house the raised beds and small border will be planted with spring and summer hardy annuals to give year round interest.

paul dracott garden designs

THE DESIGNER APPROACH

The Outline Planting Scheme prepared by Paul Dracott is shown below — the reason why he has chosen the various bed and border types is explained. In addition a Detailed Planting Scheme for the west-facing herbaceous border (6) is included to show how designers present individual bed and border schemes.

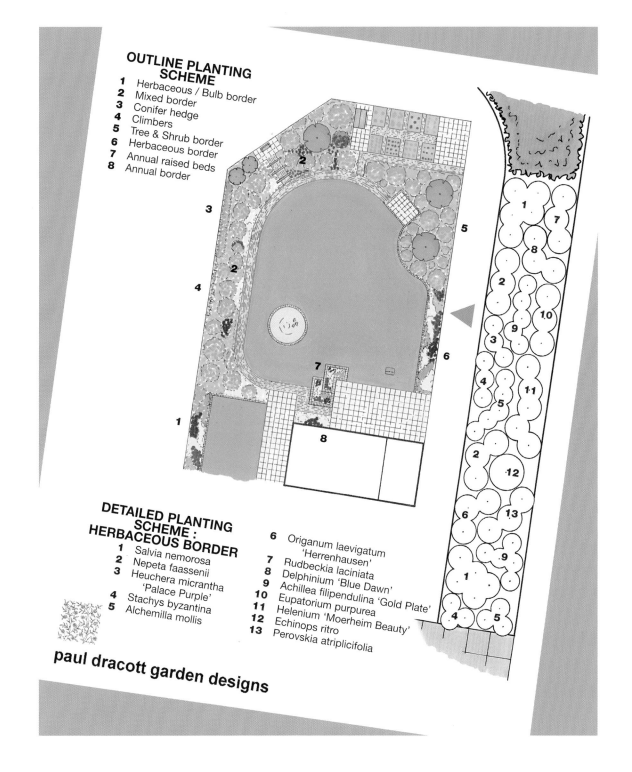

OUTLINE PLANTING SCHEME

1 Herbaceous / Bulb border
2 Mixed border
3 Conifer hedge
4 Climbers
5 Tree & Shrub border
6 Herbaceous border
7 Annual raised beds
8 Annual border

DETAILED PLANTING SCHEME : HERBACEOUS BORDER

1 Salvia nemorosa
2 Nepeta faassenii
3 Heuchera micrantha 'Palace Purple'
4 Stachys byzantina
5 Alchemilla mollis
6 Origanum laevigatum 'Herrenhausen'
7 Rudbeckia laciniata
8 Delphinium 'Blue Dawn'
9 Achillea filipendulina 'Gold Plate'
10 Eupatorium purpurea
11 Helenium 'Moerheim Beauty'
12 Echinops ritro
13 Perovskia atriplicifolia

paul dracott garden designs

THE DIY APPROACH

The guidelines below should help you to plan your new garden or new border. At the outset you should follow the most important rule of all — never buy a collection of plants because you like them at the garden centre and then try to find a home for them. Plan first on paper — buy later.

1: Prepare an outline scheme

The outline scheme covers the whole garden and it shows the structural planting. This includes trees and large shrubs, climbers on walls, arches, pergolas etc and any new hedges you propose to introduce. The planting plans for beds and borders are not included in this outline scheme.

Have a list of candidate plants before you begin. This will include 'must-haves' and old favourites. Include some unusual ones by all means, but avoid the danger of a garden filled with rarities unless you are a keen plantsman. Remember that the common-or-garden ones are generally the most reliable.

Start your scheme with one of the photocopies from Step 7 which will contain the plants which are to remain. With a pencil mark up the position of the trees, shrubs and hedges which you plan to have in your new garden. Check the expected height and spread at maturity of each variety and also check that its soil and light requirements are right for the situation. A small cross or dot is used to indicate where the stem of a tree or shrub will be and a ring is drawn round it to show the anticipated spread of the plant when mature. Where there are to be several specimens of the variety as with a hedge, draw an outline of the expected mature shape and put dots or crosses within to represent the planting stations. Check that you have followed the good design rules on pages 100 - 104 — make any changes before inking in the plant symbols.

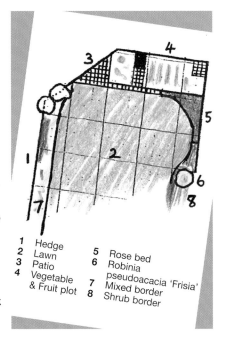

1	Hedge	5	Rose bed
2	Lawn	6	Robinia
3	Patio		pseudoacacia 'Frisia'
4	Vegetable	7	Mixed border
	& Fruit plot	8	Shrub border

2: Prepare detailed schemes

It is now time to prepare detailed schemes for the beds and borders. For each area draw its shape on a piece of graph paper — the scale will, of course, be greater than the one used for the outline scheme.

Follow the same convention — circles for individual plants, and overall spread areas where a large number of the same variety is to be planted. Use interlocking circles where a small number of herbaceous perennials is to be planted. Write the name of each plant next to each circle if not too many plants are involved — for a large bed or border it is usually better to give each circle a number and then have a separate plant list. Finally you may wish to colour the circles and areas to indicate the flower or leaf colour.

Planning a successful border takes a lot of thought. The tallest plants are generally at the back and the smallest at the front, but there should be some variation to avoid an over-regimented look. Be careful not to choose too many different types — herbaceous perennials should be planted in groups of three to five, not singly. It is age-old advice to go through your proposed list and cross out half of them.

Leaving sufficient space between the plants on your plan is another important point — see page 14 for herbaceous perennial advice and page 50 for trees and shrubs. Following these rules means that there will be an empty feel for a few years — you can overcome this by temporary planting with some cheap shrubs or annuals and bulbs. Once you have finished take photocopies of both the outline scheme and the detailed ones — you will need them once you start work.

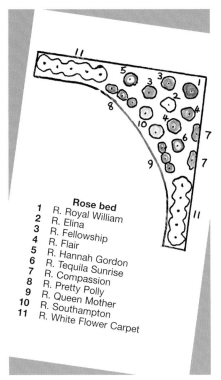

Rose bed

1	R. Royal William
2	R. Elina
3	R. Fellowship
4	R. Flair
5	R. Hannah Gordon
6	R. Tequila Sunrise
7	R. Compassion
8	R. Pretty Polly
9	R. Queen Mother
10	R. Southampton
11	R. White Flower Carpet

STEP 9 | NOW GET TO WORK

The Design Plan and Planting Scheme are finished and it is now time to begin work if the season and weather are right. The plans may have been prepared by a person or company which will be responsible for the creation of the new garden and so there is nothing more for you to do, but for most people this final step calls for a decision.

You will most likely have prepared your own design or you may have used the service of a professional — you must now decide who is going to carry out the actual work. Having to begin from scratch can be really hard work, and there is a lot to be said for using a landscape contractor if you can afford it. These people know where to go for materials, plants and so on, and they have the necessary equipment, skill and experience to do the work. You may not have the money to hand the whole job over, but do consider using a landscaper for the most strenuous parts of the project such as levelling, paving, bricklaying etc.

Pick your landscaper with care — mistakes at the garden-making stage cannot be simply rubbed out and changed like faults at the design stage. Personal recommendation is best — ask your designer if you used one, your local garden centre or a friend who has been satisfied with the work done by a contractor. Get more than one quote (fixed price, not estimate) and check a job they have done, their membership of a trade body and the cover provided by their insurance. Make sure you know exactly what is included in the quote. Fix a start date, and hand over all the plans well before that time.

For most people creating a new garden is a DIY job. Professional help may be too expensive, the garden may be very small or only a part of it may have to be changed. Whatever the reason for doing it yourself, forget the 48-hour makeover miracles you see on TV. Creating a garden is a lengthy job which may well take more than one season. It is usual to begin at the back of the garden, then the sides and finally the front garden. Don't try to do everything at once — tackle the work in a logical order. Listed below is a standard sequel of events followed by landscape contractors.

Garden making step by step

1. **SITE CLEARANCE** Remove builders' rubble in a brand new garden — unwanted trees and shrubs etc in a garden to be changed.

2. **EARTHWORKS** Establish new levels if necessary. Remember that topsoil must never be buried — move it away for later use.

3. **MARKING OUT** The distances shown on the plans must be translated to the garden and the areas marked out accordingly. Use canes and white string. If you have a change of heart when working on the site, make sure that the plan is altered.

4. **WALL & FENCE BUILDING**

5. **PAVING** First lay down lighting cables and water pipes if they are to be installed.

6. **SOIL PREPARATION** Beds and borders need levelling — bring in topsoil if necessary. Allow soil to settle.

7. **PLANTING** Now is the time for putting in the trees, shrubs and herbaceous perennials.

8. **LAWN AREA PREPARATION** Level — prepare surface for seeding or turf laying. Allow soil to settle.

9. **GRASSING** Sow grass seed or put down turves.

HARD LANDSCAPING HINTS

Laying bricks

The first job is to use pegs with string stretched tightly between them to mark out the width of the foundation trench. Dig out the earth to the depth and width shown below. If the bottom of the trench is not firm, remove the soft earth and replace with hardcore.

Pour in concrete to the recommended depth and leave to set for at least 4 days. Spread a 1 cm thick layer of mortar along the concrete and lay the first brick. Lay a second brick 6 brick-lengths away — use a straightedge and spirit level to check the level. Repeat until the far end is reached — lay additional bricks to fill in the gaps between the widely-spaced bricks. Check both vertical and horizontal levels regularly.

(1) Spread a 1 cm thick layer of mortar over about 3 bricks

(2) Press down brick. Scrape off excess mortar

(3) 'Butter' 1 cm thick layer of mortar on to head of next brick

(4) Press down brick so that it is firmly bedded below and on the buttered side. Scrape off excess mortar. Check horizontal level. Tap with trowel handle if necessary

(5) Check vertical level with straightedge. Tap side of brick with trowel handle if necessary

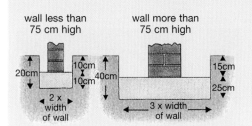

wall less than 75 cm high

wall more than 75 cm high

20cm 10cm 40cm 15cm 10cm 25cm

2 x width of wall

3 x width of wall

Erecting fence panels

Erect a post ① and then attach a panel to it. Support this panel on bricks ②. Now erect the next post at the other end of the panel — again fix the panel to the post as shown ③. Attach the next panel to this post, supporting it with the bricks removed from the previous section ④. Carry on with this post-panel-post-panel-post routine ⑤ until the fence is finished.

Metal post spikes are an easy-to-use alternative to digging holes. Place a wood block in the cup and hammer into the ground. Remove block and insert post when only the cup is visible.

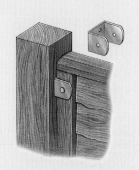

or

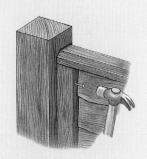

Panel clips avoid the problem of frame splitting which occurs when nailing is done badly

Nailing is the traditional method. Three 75 mm long galvanized nails are needed

Laying paving slabs

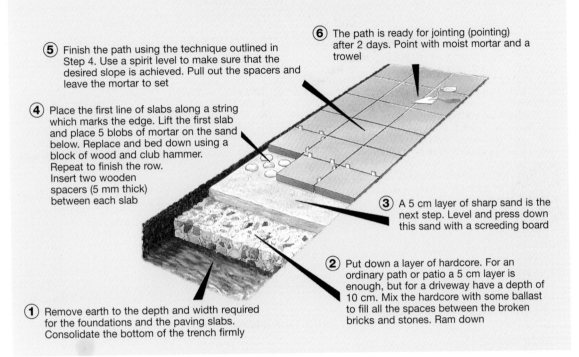

⑤ Finish the path using the technique outlined in Step 4. Use a spirit level to make sure that the desired slope is achieved. Pull out the spacers and leave the mortar to set

⑥ The path is ready for jointing (pointing) after 2 days. Point with moist mortar and a trowel

④ Place the first line of slabs along a string which marks the edge. Lift the first slab and place 5 blobs of mortar on the sand below. Replace and bed down using a block of wood and club hammer. Repeat to finish the row. Insert two wooden spacers (5 mm thick) between each slab

③ A 5 cm layer of sharp sand is the next step. Level and press down this sand with a screeding board

② Put down a layer of hardcore. For an ordinary path or patio a 5 cm layer is enough, but for a driveway have a depth of 10 cm. Mix the hardcore with some ballast to fill all the spaces between the broken bricks and stones. Ram down

① Remove earth to the depth and width required for the foundations and the paving slabs. Consolidate the bottom of the trench firmly

Building steps

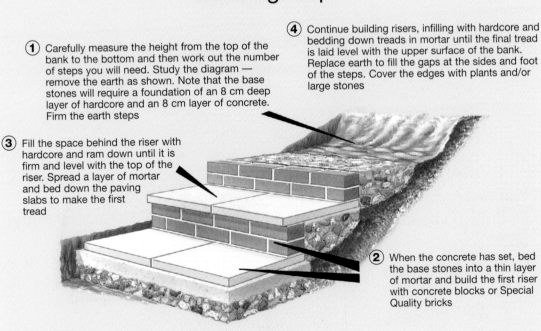

① Carefully measure the height from the top of the bank to the bottom and then work out the number of steps you will need. Study the diagram — remove the earth as shown. Note that the base stones will require a foundation of an 8 cm deep layer of hardcore and an 8 cm layer of concrete. Firm the earth steps

④ Continue building risers, infilling with hardcore and bedding down treads in mortar until the final tread is laid level with the upper surface of the bank. Replace earth to fill the gaps at the sides and foot of the steps. Cover the edges with plants and/or large stones

③ Fill the space behind the riser with hardcore and ram down until it is firm and level with the top of the riser. Spread a layer of mortar and bed down the paving slabs to make the first tread

② When the concrete has set, bed the base stones into a thin layer of mortar and build the first riser with concrete blocks or Special Quality bricks

Acknowledgements

The author wishes to acknowledge the painstaking work of Gill Jackson and Angelina Gibbs. Grateful acknowledgement is also made for the help received from Barry Highland (Spot On Digital Imaging Ltd), Paul Dracott (Paul Dracott Garden Design Ltd), Brian O'Shea and Tony Brundell.

The author is also grateful for the photographs and/or artworks received from David Baylis, Dr Tim Baylis, Julia Boulton (Gardening Which?), © Garden Matters, © Garden Matters/Milkins, © Garden Matters/Parks, Garden World Images, David Guthrie/Bluebridge Farm Studio, Michael Warren/Photos Horticultural, Janis Wales (Gardening Which?) and Christine Wilson.